Girls Camp

made easy

Girls Camp

made easy

Vickie Hacking

CFI
Springville, Utah

ISBN 13: 978-1-59955-121-0

Published by CFI, an imprint of Cedar Fort, Inc., 2373 W. 700 S., Springville, UT, 84663
Distributed by Cedar Fort, Inc., www.cedarfort.com

Cover design by Angela Olsen
Cover design © 2008 by Lyle Mortimer
Edited and typeset by Annaliese B. Cox

Printed in the United States of America

10 9 8 7 6 5 4 3 2 1

Printed on acid-free paper

When a leader is organized before camp,
her mind is at peace, and she has the
time and strength to concentrate on her
relationship with each of her young women.

Contents

Acknowledgments

I would like to thank my dear husband, Carl, for his continued support of my work in the Girls Camp program. He has had many opportunities to spend extra time with our four children, thanks to my Young Women callings. I am deeply indebted to him for being so lovingly patient as I fulfill my dream of writing a book about Girls Camp.

To my daughters, Jasmine and Hailey, may you know of my love for this inspired program. I hope that you come to love it as much as I do.

To all the Young Women leaders, for whom this book was written, may you enjoy life as a leader, as it is a lifelong calling, even when you get released. Your teachings really do stick with the young women you serve. They are forever grateful for you.

I would also like to acknowledge the wonderful woman who served so diligently as my Young Women president—Jeanne Baker, thank you for all your guidance and friendship at a very crucial time in my life. This one's for you!

I would not be where I am today without the Girls Camp program. I feel that Girls Camp is one of the most inspired programs in the Church. What better place to be such an influence in the lives of the youth than in the beautiful surroundings that God made for us! I want all you Young Women who I have had the privilege of serving—whether it was in Utah, Florida, or Oklahoma—to know how wonderful you are. You are the ones who inspire me to do good. Plan now—you are the camp leaders of tomorrow.

Introduction

I remember being a new twelve-year-old Beehive and packing my bags for a week at Girls Camp. I had no idea what was in store for me: how much my testimony would grow, my physical strength would increase, and my friendships would develop. I would never have guessed that I would instantly fall in love with this awesome program. Of course, I liked camping; my family would go camping every summer, sometimes more than once. But Girls Camp was different. We hiked, canoed, built campfires, and ate delicious Dutch oven meals, but there was something there that wasn't there when my family camped. It was my Young Women leaders and all my friends. I still thank my Heavenly Father for blessing me with such terrific leaders, specifically Jeannie Baker and Becky Tyler.

There is a need for a Girls Camp book that teaches about all aspects of the camp program because so many women get called as camp directors who have never been to Girls Camp before and who are given very little direction. I hope that through this book, women everywhere will feel more confident in their wonderful callings as Young Women leaders, specifically camp directors.

Each section is filled with ideas. You do not need to follow these as they are listed; they're merely suggestions. You and your fellow Young Women leaders should come up with the final plan for your camp. Think about your young women who you serve and the needs they have. Prayerfully plan your activities, and seek the guidance of our Heavenly Father.

I wish I could come and sit down with you and tell you all about my experiences at Girls Camp. I hope you get a feel for how much respect I have for this program. I love the Young Women program and care deeply for the youth of the Church. Girls Camp is an inspired addition to the basics of the Young Women program. I hold it close to my heart in every respect.

I want to give a special thank you to all the sisters who submitted their camp themes. It is nice to know that camp leaders throughout the Church know how to have fun yet are still able to concentrate on strengthening the young women's testimonies.

If it weren't for the leaders who taught me how to lash together a chair, or to properly clean and season a Dutch oven, I would never have grown to love Girls Camp like I do. This is why I am so passionate about sharing just a little bit of this knowledge with you. Leaders really do make or break a week at camp. I hope that all of you wonderful leaders will take the time to prayerfully prepare to spend this glorious week with your young women. They are counting on you for guidance, friendship, and love. Teach them to walk in the light of his love, and they will return that love to you and to their families. I pray that all of you leaders will spiritually prepare for this experience you are about to embark upon. You will learn and grow with the girls if you do.

Good luck to all of you. May the young women you serve feel your burning desire to strengthen your own testimony, as well as theirs, through your leadership and example of your love for our Savior Jesus Christ.

I would love to hear about your experiences at Girls Camp. You can reach me at ywsuggestions@yahoo.com.

① Planning

When women first get called as camp directors, most are overwhelmed thinking about all the things they will need to do. *Calm down!* Camp should be fun for you too! If you plan ahead and prepare spiritually, you will have the time of your life.

Here is a checklist of basic information that is needed to start preparing for Girls Camp. Arrange and plan according to the needs of the young women in your ward or stake.

Planning Checklist

- ☐ Call an assistant camp director.
- ☐ Ask to be included in other Young Women activities so you are able to get to know the girls before going to camp with them. They will respond to you better if they know you before attending camp.
- ☐ Hold meetings with your ward or stake Young Women presidency at least once a month, beginning six months prior to camp.
- ☐ Plan with a purpose—you want camp to be memorable and a growing experience for all who attend. Make a checklist of all the things you need to plan and carry out: get a list of young women attending camp, get information to parents and girls at least three months in advance, make permission slips, work with youth camp leaders (YCLs), decide on a theme, budget finances, plan pre-camp activities, schedule transportation to and from camp, create camp decorations, plan

camp activities (devotionals, campfires, flag ceremonies, bishopric and testimony nights, etc.), make song books, plan menu, purchase cooking supplies, make first-aid kits, come up with craft and award ideas, plan hikes, and prepare for certification.

☐ Get ahold of a stake Girls Camp schedule as soon as possible. Find out the stake theme and plan yours around it. Decide on the theme as soon as possible, including daily themes. Base the daily themes around your weekly theme. Planning themes early will help you successfully plan theme-related activities at camp. This also gets the young women excited about coming to camp.

☐ Delegate the spiritual hikes, scripture study time, and evening devotionals to the Young Women president; she is responsible for the spiritual aspect of camp.

☐ Delegate responsibilities to other members of the Young Women presidency and the assistant camp director. They need to be involved and can help you plan a successful camp. Some things that could be delegated to others are food, certification, skits, roll calls, money collection, permission slips, and music. Don't try to do it all.

☐ Do some of the certification at pre-camp activities. You may want to plan a first-aid day that teaches the required certification information prior to camp. See if your stake would like to plan it with you.

☐ Plan your days at camp carefully. Leave time in the schedule for occasional free time. But be careful: too much to do or too much free time can make a camp restless and irritable. Separate strenuous activities with some down time in between.

☐ After camp, evaluate your camp experience. Let it be a teaching tool for next year.

Individual Checklist
for girls and leaders

Each individual should bring these items to camp. Some items can be shared, like whetstones, triangular bandages, and so forth. All clothing taken to camp should be practical, comfortable, modest, and rugged enough to withstand rigorous camping activities.

Suggested Clothing Items

- ☐ pajamas
- ☐ bathrobe (optional)
- ☐ socks
- ☐ 2 pairs of shoes (1 pair sturdy enough for hiking; no open-toed or high-heel shoes)
- ☐ underwear
- ☐ shirts (1 long-sleeved)
- ☐ pants (2 or more)
- ☐ hat
- ☐ sweater, warm jacket, or coat
- ☐ work gloves
- ☐ poncho, raincoat, or water-repellent jacket
- ☐ thermal underwear (optional)
- ☐ swim suit (optional)

General Accessories

- ☐ *Young Women Camp Manual*
- ☐ scriptures
- ☐ Personal Progress book
- ☐ journal (or notebook) and pen
- ☐ flashlight (with fresh batteries)
- ☐ compass
- ☐ eating utensils or mess kit
- ☐ musical instrument (optional)
- ☐ inexpensive camera with extra film (or a disposable camera)
- ☐ rope
- ☐ pocketknife and whetstone

- ☐ canteen (for hikes)
- ☐ backpack (for hikes)
- ☐ triangular bandage (or bandana)
- ☐ gifts for secret sister or secret ward

Suggested Bedding

- ☐ sleeping bag or bedroll
- ☐ quilt or extra blanket
- ☐ pillow and pillow case
- ☐ ground cover (tarp or old shower curtain)

Toilet Accessories

- ☐ wash cloth
- ☐ towels (bath and face)
- ☐ sewing kit (including scissors)
- ☐ soap and shower gel
- ☐ sanitary needs
- ☐ toilet paper
- ☐ nail file and cleaner
- ☐ comb and brush
- ☐ toothbrush and toothpaste
- ☐ facial tissue
- ☐ first-aid kit (including insect repellent)

Equipment Checklist

for ward or stake leaders

This list can be modified according to your camp's needs. Check with your stake to see what individual wards will need to provide for themselves.

menu chart/recipes
job chart
pots and pans (including fry pans, soup kettles, and dish pans)
grills
Dutch ovens
propane stoves
mixing bowls
gloves or hot pads
measuring spoons/cups
cooking utensils (long handles)
knives (butcher and paring)
graters
peelers
tongs
spatulas
wire whisk
hangers
roasters
cutting boards
can openers
plastic pitchers
serving bowls
serving trays
serving utensils
tablecloths

paper napkins, plates, cups, and plastic utensils
ziplock bags
plastic wrap
wax paper
aluminum foil
garbage bags
paper towels
ice
water jugs
cooking/heating water
coolers
portable kitchen box
dish cloths/towels
brillo pads
scrub brush
dish detergent
bleach
hand washing basin
buckets
soap
fingernail brush
broom and dustpan
toilet paper
briquettes
wood
newspaper
fine steel wool

matches
tarp for woodpile
tarp for shade
tents for supplies
clock
insect repellent
lanterns
first-aid kit
tin snips
file
wire
twine/rope
hammer
rake
shovel
ax/hatchet
saw
whetstone
pliers
needle and thread
clothespins
certification materials
arts/crafts supplies
masking tape
tacks
duct tape

Other items:
_____
_____

Camp Fund-raisers

We all know that Girls Camp can get pricey, especially for families that have more than one daughter attending. Fund-raising can be a successful way to help every girl pay for and attend camp. Keep in mind that not all wards or stakes encourage or approve of fund-raisers. Be sure to check with your bishopric on the policy in your area.

Before you plan a fund-raiser, determine how much money you will need to make and then plan accordingly. All fund-raisers take time, planning, and preparation. Two of the most important keys to a successful fund-raiser are advertising and location. Be creative and *involve the girls* in choosing a fund-raiser. This is their fund-raiser, so put them to work. Below is a list of ideas for fund-raisers. Prices are not listed, so you can determine what needs to be earned depending on your own circumstances. Asking for donations is an alternative to charging a set amount for any given service you are providing.

garage sale	washing windows	house work for elderly
running errands	family portraits	cultural dinner and auction
babysitting	silent auction	Mother's Day bouquets
gift baskets	bake sale	first-aid kits for cars
car wash	recycling	Valentine's Day love notes
ward breakfast	craft boutique	group babysitting
72-hour kits	gift wrapping	Young Women cookbook

Another idea is to save your change—it adds up quickly. Have a jar outside the Young Women room where girls, leaders, and ward members can contribute. You could also set up a refreshment booth at local school sporting events. Purchase the goodies at warehouse stores like Costco for a better price.

Arranging Pre-Camp Activities

Successful pre-camp activities are a huge help in planning and preparing for camp. You can use these activities to do some of the certification before camp, to have the girls help plan some aspects of camp (especially girls who will be YCLs), and to have the girls help in making decorations or other things needed for camp.

When planning pre-camp activities, start as early as possible. The camp director should arrange to attend a Young Women presidency meeting in December or January. Work with the presidency to schedule pre-camp activities during Mutual or on Saturdays. Plan your activities around what you need to get accomplished. You will feel so good when you see camp starting to come together.

Pre-Camp Activities Timeline

1. Decide how many pre-camp activities it will take to accomplish all you need to get done prior to camp.
2. Plan your first activity. In this activity, announce the theme, dates of camp, cost, and so forth. You may want to invite parents to this meeting.
3. Have regular pre-camp activities, starting in February or March. This will give you plenty of time to accomplish all that needs to be done before camp.
4. Plan for more pre-camp activities in the month or two before camp. You may want to have a few Saturday morning activities to work on more time consuming items, like making camp decorations or first-aid kits.

Attendance

Those Who Should Come to Camp

1. Girls who have completed the sixth grade in school or are between the ages of twelve and eighteen. Check with local priesthood leaders for rules in your area pertaining to girls who have not turned twelve by the camp dates but have completed the sixth grade.
2. Assigned adult leaders such as the camp director, assistant, Young Women presidency, and advisors.
3. Bishopric and their wives on bishopric night.

Send out invitations to bishopric members and less active girls. Have all the young women sign the invitation so the less active girls know that their peers are encouraging them to come, not just the leaders. Encourage the bishopric to attend as much as they can. The girls really love having someone there to impress. You will also want the whole bishopric, along with their wives, to come up on testimony night.

Those Who Should Not Come

1. No young men under eighteen years of age.
2. No unmarried priesthood leaders.
3. No friends of either the youth or adult leaders who just want to visit.

Late Arrival and Early Departure

Occasionally there will be girls who will need to arrive or depart from camp at a different time than the rest. Allow them to do this only if it is necessary. Don't let them leave just because they are not having fun. Make note of these *prior* to camp. When camping as a stake, let the stake leaders know if any of your girls are arriving late or departing early; this will help them keep a count of who is there.

Rules

This list of rules can be applied to any Girls Camp. Of course, they may need to be modified for your certain stake or ward rules. Be aware of the surroundings of your camp and adjust these rules as needed. Some camp sites allow things that others do not. Adjust these rules so they will follow along with your designated camp and its rules.

Location

Rules need to be made according to the camp's location. For example: if you are staying in a lodge where you have electricity, hair dryers and curling irons may be allowed; if you have access to a pool or lake, swimming may be allowed. If you are camping in rugged areas, then there would be no need for such items. Also on the basis of where you are, pregnant leaders may or may not be allowed to come.

General Policies

All young women and leaders must abide by these rules while at camp.

1. *Church standards must be observed at all times.*
2. Girls must have respect for other people's property—buses, camp facilities, and so forth—and especially respect for one another.
3. Certified adult leaders and qualified YCLs will be the only ones qualified to certify the girls.

4. Girls are not allowed to drive to and from camp.
5. Girls should not bring mp3 players, face cards, handheld video games, cell phones, and so forth to camp.
6. Do not bring *anything* that will detract from the Spirit.

While at Camp

1. No initiation or hazing!
2. Carry out camp assignments with a cheerful attitude.
3. Keep the campsite clean. Each girl must be responsible for her share of the chores at camp.
4. *All girls must hike.* If there is a physical problem or disability, a horizontal hike should be provided.

Discipline

Who Should Discipline

Discipline at Girls Camp should be left up to the ward or stake Young Women president, or her counselors when she is not available. If this is not possible or effective, the most serious circumstances should be handled with the help of the presiding priesthood leaders.

Minor Problems

Some minor situations can be solved peacefully by calmly thinking things through. For example, if a young woman chooses to bring an item to camp that is not permitted, say an iPod, simply take it away and return it to her after she has arrived home at the conclusion of camp. If the problem arises where a girl is leaving the designated camp area or arranging to meet boys during the Girls Camp period, limit her unsupervised time and assign her a buddy. The buddy system should always be obeyed at Girls Camp anyway.

Repeat Offenders

When rules are continually being broken by the same young woman or group of young women, send them home. They must abide by the camp rules in order to participate. If problems continue to occur, prayerfully counsel with your bishop and the parents of the troublesome young women. You want all the young women in your ward or stake to have the blessings of Girls Camp. Do everything in your power to allow these girls to participate without giving them the feeling that they have been singled out.

Who Should Know

When discipline situations do arise, keep it between the young woman involved and the leaders. Don't announce to the camp who is causing trouble. No young woman wants her peers to know she has made a mistake.

Be Positive

Allow the young woman to correct her mistake if possible. Accept an apology and move on, keeping the camp peaceful and joyous. Keep a positive attitude—it's contagious. Camp rules need to be obeyed, but be prepared for when they are not.

Work Groups

When planning work groups, you need at least three separate groups: meal prep, cleanup, and making fires. You can assign them one of two ways: a new group for each meal *or* the same group for the whole day. When assigning who is in each group, include leaders and young women from each level of certification. The YCLs can help teach the younger girls. You may need to assign different types of work depending on your camp location.

Assignments by Day

It is often easier to have the same work group assigned for the whole day rather than each meal. The young women tend to remember better when they are responsible for an assignment the whole day.

If fires are prohibited, replace the fire group with another responsibility. If your meals are cooked for you, have the cooking committee help gather the girls.

Monday	Tuesday	Wednesday	Thursday
Meal prep: Group 1	Meal prep: 3	Meal prep: 2	Meal prep: 1
Cleanup: Group 2	Cleanup: 1	Cleanup: 3	Cleanup: 2
Fires: Group 3	Fires: 2	Fires: 1	Fires: 3

Assignments by Meal

Assign a different group to each meal so that everyone will have a chance to help in each area.

Monday	**Tuesday**	**Wednesday**	**Thursday**
Breakfast	**Breakfast**	**Breakfast**	**Breakfast**
Meal prep: Group 1	Meal prep: 3	Meal prep: 2	Meal prep: 1
Cleanup: Group 2	Cleanup: 1	Cleanup: 3	Cleanup: 2
Fires: Group 3	Fires: 2	Fires: 1	Fires: 3
Lunch	**Lunch**	**Lunch**	**Lunch**
Meal prep: 3	Meal prep: 2	Meal prep: 1	Meal prep: 3
Cleanup: 1	Cleanup: 3	Cleanup: 2	Cleanup: 1
Fires: 2	Fires: 1	Fires: 3	Fires: 2
Dinner	**Dinner**	**Dinner**	**Dinner**
Meal prep: 2	Meal prep: 1	Meal prep: 3	Meal prep: 2
Cleanup: 3	Cleanup: 2	Cleanup: 1	Cleanup: 3
Fires: 1	Fires: 3	Fires: 2	Fires: 1

Camp Schedule

On the following pages is a sample camp schedule. The italicized activities are stake events. Most activities won't take up the entire allotted time.

Time	Day 1	Day 2
7 AM	load buses at stake center	wake up!
8 AM	arrive at camp	breakfast and cleanup
9 AM	set up camp	*flag*
10 AM	ward welcome	*waterfront* (canoes and swimming)
11 AM	*welcome and flag*	certification
12 PM	lunch and cleanup	(continued)
1 PM	spiritual hike	lunch and cleanup
2 PM	craft time	spiritual hike
3 PM	certification and dinner prep	skit prep
4 PM	(continued)	certification, skit prep, and dinner prep
5 PM	dinner and cleanup	dinner and cleanup
6 PM	compass course	6:30 stake skits
7 PM	confidence courses	(continued)
8 PM	*lowering of flag*	*lowering of flag*
9 PM	campfire	campfire
10 PM	late night snack	late night snack
11 PM	lights out!	lights out!

Time	Day 3	Day 4	Day 5
7 AM	wake up!	wake up!	5:45 AM wake up! cabin cleanup (all bags must be ready to go before eating breakfast)
8 AM	breakfast and cleanup	breakfast and cleanup	
9 AM	flag	flag	
10 AM	prepare sack lunches for hikes	9:30 AM certification (must be done by today)	
11 AM	hikes		7 AM breakfast and cleanup
12 PM	(continued)	lunch and cleanup	8 AM load buses
1 PM	(continued)	*waterfront games*	10 AM arrive home
2 PM	(continued)	spiritual hike	
3 PM	craft time	workshop with stake president	
4 PM	certification and dinner prep	dinner prep and cabin cleanup	
5 PM	dinner and cleanup	dinner and cleanup with bishopric and wives	
6 PM	spiritual hike	(continued)	
7 PM	flag retirement ceremony	testimony meeting	
8 PM	campfire	(continued)	
9 PM	stake singing time around lake	(continued)	
10 PM	late night snack	late night snack	
11 PM	lights out!	lights out!	

Flag Ceremonies

When camping as a ward or stake, it is helpful to have a morning and evening flag ceremony to provide a time to give instruction for the current day's events, to start the day off with some silliness, and to teach the girls how to properly present a flag ceremony and how to behave during one. This is the perfect setting for the YCLs to show what they are made of. They should be the ones up front, leading the group in song. YCLs should conduct the flag ceremonies each morning and night, and each ward or group should have an opportunity to present or retire the flag. This is the YCLs' time to learn leadership, and the younger girls will look up to them.

It will take awhile to gather everyone for a flag ceremony, so plan to sing camp songs until everyone has arrived. Begin with upbeat, active songs and end with mellow or spiritual songs.

How to Fold a Flag

To properly fold a flag, begin by holding it waist-high with another person so that its surface is parallel to the ground.

1. Fold lengthwise.
2. Fold lengthwise again.
3. Fold striped corner over till it meets the edge.
4. Keep folding in triangles until only the blue star field is showing. Tuck end into flag.

Morning Flag Ceremony

- Plan to have the morning flag ceremony as early as possible. When it drags on into the midmorning hours, the girls and leaders get restless and the heat of the day can be a distraction. Nine o'clock is a good time. This leaves plenty of time in the morning to eat before coming and enough time afterward to squeeze in an activity before lunch.
- Once everyone has arrived, have regular opening exercises, including song, prayer, Young Women theme, and a scripture or spiritual thought.
- Present and raise the flag. Make sure that all the girls who need to certify this requirement have a turn to help.
- Say the Pledge of Allegiance.
- Have a patriotic thought or story, ending with a patriotic song.
- You could present a skit or short program introducing the daily camp theme or reiterating the weekly theme.

- Make announcements briefly detailing where everyone needs to be and when.
- Make sure the morning flag ceremony does not take up too much time; fifteen to twenty minutes is plenty. The girls and leaders want to get on with their day and all the wonderful things planned.

Evening Flag Ceremony

- Open with a song and a prayer.
- Lower the flag. Make sure that all the girls who need to certify this requirement have a turn to help.
- Have a patriotic thought or story, ending with a patriotic song.
- You may want to end here, or take time to have a nightly event, such as skits, stake singing time, a message from the stake president, guest speaker, and so forth.
- Leave enough time for individual wards to have their own campfires at their camp.

Evening Campfires

Each night at camp, leave time for an evening campfire as a ward (or if the girls are grouped by levels, then have an evening campfire for each level). YCLs can take turns conducting this meeting. The outline for an evening campfire can vary from night to night. You may want to have a reverent devotional time, get-to-know-you games, skits, or singing time. You should always plan to have a testimony meeting as the evening camp-fire on the last night of camp.

Evening campfires should be a teaching time to reiterate the camp theme. This is a time when all your young women are gathered together around a warm glowing fire. There is no better time to teach of our Savior's love than now. Marvelous things will happen when these campfires are prepared through prayer and inspiration.

② Themes

Deciding on a theme should be the first priority for every camp leader. Everything seems to fall into place once a theme has been decided on. Themes should be spiritual *and* fun. What would camp be without a few good laughs?

Got Worth?

Focus on becoming an eight-cow woman (a spin-off from the movie *Johnny Lingo*). Open the week with a portrayal of Johnny Lingo coming into the camp in a canoe (if you are camped near a lake). Have this guest speak with the girls briefly about inner beauty and what makes an eight-cow wife (inner beauty, not outer). The stake and ward Young Women leaders could dress up like cows to kick off the theme. The camp T-shirts could be a simple pink shirt with the words "Got Worth?" and eight cows underneath it. During the week, hold a special "Moo'ow" (luau). Have each group make a cow for the table centerpieces. At the Moo'ow, have lip-syncing, karaoke, and teach a Hawaiian dance.

Survivor

In a knock-off of the TV show *Survivor*, teach the girls how to survive in this world—living *in* the world but not *of* the world. Each group should have a tribe name and a cheer. As the groups are coming together, either for flag ceremony or other group activity, have them chant their cheer: "Let me see you, kangaroo," "What's that you say?" "Let me see you, kangaroo,"

"What's that you say?" "Ooh, aah aah aah ooh, aah aah aah ooh." Fun decorations could include kangaroos, tribal material, Australian (down under) décor, and bandanas. Have each young woman paint a container to look tribal. This will be used as their mailboxes. Use wooden anchors to hang these. On a daily basis, give each person a challenge that they will need to complete that day. Tiki torches and huts can be used for decorations. The stake or ward flag ceremonies can be called Tribal Council. Each day have a reward challenge for fun items like pencils, stickers, paper, charms, visors, food, lip gloss, hair elastics, soap, beads, and so forth.

P.I.T. (Princesses In Training)

The camp area is called the P.I.T.—Princesses In Training. Each ward or group can have a different fictional princess as their theme. Try to focus each princess around a Young Women value. Decorations could include crowns, castles, and so forth. Workshops and devotionals could emphasize qualities we should obtain as heirs to the kingdom of heaven. To add variety to your hike, have stops along the way and discuss how each of the values will help the princesses train successfully. Hand out a jewel for each value color and have the young women glue the jewels onto their crowns. When the bishopric comes to visit the camp, have a jousting tournament or other medieval challenges.

Bee Keepers

Focus on the Be's from a talk given by Gordon B. Hinckley, November 2000: be grateful, be smart, be clean, be true, be humble, be prayerful. Decorations could include paper cut-outs of beehives and bees on each cabin or tent (hive 1, hive 2). Each work group can be called a colony (colony 1, colony 2). The YCLs are the queen bees. Crafts could include making beeswax candles, yellow bath salts, honey candy, or taffy. Choose one Be to focus on each day as the daily theme. You may want to end with "be humble" or "be prayerful" on the last day to lead up to the testimony meeting. There are several songs that were written around these six Be's. Pick one as your camp song.

A Colorful Camping Experience

Focus on the value colors and how they pertain to nature. Create notebooks on colored paper for each of the girls with their schedule, assignments, secret sister, and other important information in it. You can alter the rules of your camp to include the value colors, for example: Please don't make us RED with anger because you brought a radio, CD player, or shorts. You'll be YELLOW with fear if you try to leave camp without approval of camp leaders. Don't make our nature critters BLUE: no chewing gum; it could be harmful to wildlife. We don't want to turn GREEN from the smells of campers, so please use the PURPLE port-a-potty. Assign each group a color. They can create a flag and a T-shirt of that color. The stake or ward leaders can do tie-dye shirts since they are responsible for all of the color groups. You could sing "The Primary Colors" and add fun verses to it that pertain to each of the seven Young Women value colors. Camp assignments can also include colors: Burgundy Breakfast Bunch; Brown Bag Brigade; Silver Supper Servers; Red, White, and Blue Crew (Flag ceremony duty); Purple Potty Patrol (bathroom duty); and Periwinkle Prayer Service (nighttime devotional). A perfect craft would be a colorful bead bracelet.

B.U.G.S. (Bringing Upright Girls to the Savior)

Devotionals and spiritual time can focus on ways that the young women can return to the Savior. You can use the initials B.U.G. for other things, such as Be Unique Girls. Assign each ward or group a bug. You could relate a value to each bug: *Faith*—fireflies; *Divine Nature*—dragonflies or beetles; *Individual Worth*—ants or ladybugs; *Knowledge*—praying mantis; *Choice and Accountability*—spiders or Mormon crickets; *Good Works*—bees; *Integrity*—butterflies. Have each camp decorate according to the bug they have chosen—black and red for lady bugs, green for grasshoppers, and so forth. Decorations can also include all kinds of plant life, pictures of bugs, and so forth. The camp shirts could coordinate with the selected bug's main color. Make bandanas from red and white gingham checkered picnic tablecloths or material. Research survival and natural habits of bugs and relate them to the young women (bees all work in a team to accomplish the goal of making honey). Use clever sayings for the various aspects at camp: *food*—grub worms, potato bugs, tomato worms, tapeworms; *prayer time*—praying mantis; *bedtime*—bed bugs and night-crawlers; *being on time*—"Don't be a draggin'-fly," "How time flies," and "Flea from sin"; *hike*—walking sticks and centipedes; *nurse*—flu bug; *swimming*—water skeeters; *bathrooms*—stink bug and dung beetles; *woodpiles*—termites; *craft classes*—doodlebugs.

E.M.T. (Eternity Means Today)

Assign each group a medical profession. The doctors can focus on spiritual health, the dentists can focus on speaking kind words, the surgeons can focus on healing and repentance, and so forth. Decorate everything like a hospital, using the red medical cross, IVs, teddybears dressed like doctors, shoe booties, face masks, and so forth. You can use scrub outfits, and each group can wear a different color. Use hospital-type bracelets to "label" everyone. You could also make name badges with their picture and the camp theme. Call your camp the LDS ER or your stake name (Park Stake Regional Hospital). Label each cabin or tent with a place in a hospital: waiting room, triage, X-ray, prenatal, ICU, and so forth.

Ship Shape

The spiritual messages for the week could focus on a course headed back to heaven—don't steer away from it. Organize your camp as if you were on a cruise ship. Go to ports each day with various activities. Hold a midnight buffet of s'mores and hot cocoa. Plan a Captured by Pirates night where each group must perform a skit or song to be released. Have a recreational director that plans and leads the groups to daily activities. Decorate pillow cases with glow-in-the-dark paint and stamps.

Olympics

The spiritual focus should be to try your best, represent your country and Church worthily wherever you go, and work hard to accomplish great things. Assign each group a country and decorate accordingly. Hold one big Olympic day with all kinds of games and events. Each night, award individuals and groups with medals for good deeds done during the day. The main lodge or gathering area can be called the Olympic Village. Decorate it with all kinds of décor from countries all over the world. T-shirts could show the Olympic rings designed with all the value colors.

Quest for the Best

The spiritual message is to be the best: look for the best in others, have the "best" kind of friends, do your best in everything you do, or face your dragons and conquer them. Name each group with a medieval theme: knights, jesters, squires, merry minstrels, jousters, ladies in waiting, royal chefs, sorcerers, castle staff, lords, and so forth. Each group could make a shield or flag to represent themselves. Kick off the week by having a knight and a lady ride through the camp on a horse; then have them give a devotional. Hold a medieval tournament with forms of jousting and knight contests. You could have a ropes course called the Dragon's Lair. Have one medieval dinner of chicken, corn on the cob, and fruit without silverware, reigned over by a queen (camp director).

Everyday Heroes

Everyone is a hero to somebody. During your daily devotionals, recount stories about women heroes from the scriptures: Eve, Ruth, Mary, Abish, and so forth. You could also discuss other heroes—historical or modern day. Each group can be a cartoon hero: Ninja Turtles, Care Bears, Superwoman, and so forth. If you plan a ropes course, call it Tarzan's Jungle. Plan a Pebbles of Perfection night hike where the superheroes are tested. Give each person a bag of bright white or glow-in-the-dark pebbles. Prepare a path that has stops along the way that each person will individually stop at. These stops will ask them a question about the Word of Wisdom, morality, honesty, and so forth. If they do well in a specific area, they keep all their pebbles; if they need to work on that area, they drop a pebble at the sign. After the hike discuss how they can work on keeping more of their pebbles.

B.O.O.T Camp (Be Of One Troop, Build On Our Testimonies, Building Our Own Testimonies)

Focus on building strong testimonies. Everybody in the camp could wear camouflage shirts and dog tags (ask your local reserve office to donate some dog tags). Name each group or level a different rank: general, sergeant, soldier, commander, and so forth. Name all of your events like the army: *games*—night maneuvers; *lodge*—mess hall; *talent show or skits*—USO show; *orientation*—basic training. Daily themes could be Back to Basics; Carry On; When the Going Gets Tough, the Tough Get Going; Espirit de Corp (spirit of camaraderie); The Few, The Proud, The Righteous; Be All That You Can Be—In the Army of the Lord. During the week, simulate the experiences you might have if you were joining the army, but with a spiritual twist. Give the girls their "rations," items like a sweatshirt, toiletries (try asking a local hotel to donate these), a camouflage hairband, and so forth. Have everyone complete a "spiritual physical." Call the permission slips and other information sheets their military papers.

Tribes of Truth—Book of Mormon

Name each group an Indian name: Cherokee, Ute, Navajo, and so forth. Buy tall wooden poles and have each ward or group make a totem pole. Each totem pole can have a different animal on it. Each animal has certain attributes that the group can try to emulate throughout the week. Display the totem poles all week long. Give out beads for accomplishments and awards during the week. Hold a special fireside where a guest speaker comes and talks about Indian heritage. Have a Rite of Passage evening, where each girl contemplates goals she wants to achieve. The main spiritual focus is the Book of Mormon stories and doctrine.

A Chosen Generation

The main spiritual focus is that each generation of young women are chosen for their specific time. You were chosen for now. How will you represent your own chosen generation? Assign each group a different decade. For skit night, have each group perform a dance from their decade. Each group could design a T-shirt according to their decade: seventies—tie-dyed shirt, fifties—poodle skirts, and so forth. During devotionals, focus on messages that were taught by the prophet of that time. Hold a special group fireside and have prophets from each of the different decades come and teach the groups (played by bishopric or stake presidency members).

Holidays

The main spiritual focus is that there are many things to be grateful for all year long. Each is different but important. Assign each ward or group a holiday with an appropriate value color: *Easter* (white)—focus on the Resurrection, have an Easter egg hunt; *Fourth of July* (blue)—patriotism; *Valentine's Day* (red)—emphasize charity and love; *Halloween* (orange)—hold a spook alley and go trick-or-treating by giving treats instead of taking; *Thanksgiving* (yellow)—be thankful for blessings, have a turkey feast. For skits, groups can prepare a story that explains the origin of their assigned holiday.

Feast upon the Word

The main spiritual focus is to feast upon the words of Christ in the scriptures and the Church magazines. Assign each group a fast food restaurant—Burger King, Weinerschnitzel, Taco Bell, McDonald's, Wendy's and so forth. See if your local restaurants will donate cups, hats, napkins, bags, and shirts to be used at camp. Play food games, like drop the Jell-O in your mouth, run with an egg on a spoon, pie eating contest, and so forth.

Fishers of Men

The main spiritual focus of the Fishers of Men theme can be to make good friends, make wise dating and moral decisions, follow the Savior, set a good example, and share our testimony and the gospel with others. Have a special fireside where a priesthood holder comes and talks with the girls about dating. Assign each group to be a sea creature. Play several water games like water balloon volleyball, water gun war, swimming, canoeing, and so forth. Decorate with all kinds of nautical items like nets, poles, hooks, boats, and anchors. Label everyone's bed or mailbox with paper fishes labeled with their name, year of camp, and ward or group name. You could also use paper fish cutouts as the paper that you use to write notes to each other on all week. A perfect craft could be to decorate picture frames with shells, stickers, paint, fish pattern material, and so forth.

Camp-a-Lot (Where Dreams Begin)

The main spiritual focus is to help the girls understand that we are all heirs to the kingdom of heaven. Assign each group a motto. Have them design their flag accordingly. Mottos could be: Swords and Stones; Heroes and Thrones; Princesses of Potential; Princesses on Parade; Slaying the Dragon; Conquering the Foe; Prince of Peace: Our Royal Heritage; or Return with Honor. On the first night of camp, hold a knighting ceremony to knight the YCLs. During the week, hold a town fair where each group is responsible for preparing a game or activity that pertains to the theme, such as tug-of-war, jousting, photo stop (holes cut out of a cardboard box, stick your head through the hole and your face is the head of a dragon or a princess). You could hold a royal ball and teach various line dances. For the closing ceremony, hold a royal feast with a guest speaker.

Safari (Searchin' for Heaven)

Assign each ward or group a safari-type name and decorate accordingly. Daily themes could be Bear Necessities; Get Equipped, It's a Jungle Out There; Face to Face with Danger; Safari Sisters; Searching for Heaven; Come Back Home; Safari Sunsets; or Faith in Every Footstep. Have a Visiting Villages time each day where each ward or group hosts another group and prepares games, treats, or whatever they think of. This really helps the wards or groups get to know each other. Be sure to do this enough times so each group has a chance to host all the other groups. Hold a treasure hunt each day with clues that lead the girls to a hidden treasure. You could give pieces of a puzzle every day to each group, so by the end of the week they will have all the puzzle pieces needed to put together a puzzle. You could also do this as a whole stake and hand out large puzzle pieces that combine into a huge safari puzzle. If you purposely leave pieces out, it could serve as an object lesson on unity and how every young woman is needed in the stake or ward. Craft could include you teaching everyone how to make balloon animals or woven bead necklaces.

In T.U.N.E. (Testify, Unite, Navigate, Enlighten)

The spiritual focus of camp is feeling the Spirit through music. All week long focus on music. Assign each ward or group a musical. They can plan their skit, ward cheer, decorations, T-shirts, and so forth around this theme. The award ceremony after the skits can be called the Tony Awards. All handouts and invitations can be designed to look like playbills from Broadway. The camp schedule could follow this format as well. Decorate your camp like a Broadway Theater.

The Magic Kingdom

The main spiritual focus is the magic kingdom of heaven. During the week, concentrate on heavenly topics: celestial kingdom, Heavenly Father, Jesus Christ, prayer, peace and happiness, scripture study, and so forth. Assign each ward or group a Disney story to be their theme: 101 Dalmatians, Little Mermaid, Cinderella, Lion King, Hercules, and so forth. Skits can be based on these stories (the Disney story books are a great help for skits). Decorations could be clouds made from poster board with cotton balls glued on or silver glitter around the edges, pictures of Disney characters, names of the characters, rides at the Disney amusement parks, heavenly names, cut-outs in the shape of a castle, and so forth.

Care-a-Lot (Care Bears)

The main spiritual focus is serving others and letting others serve you by accepting service. Discuss the ongoing duels between good and evil. Assign a Care Bear to each ward or group. Some ideas are Bedtime Bear, Birthday Bear, Cheer Bear, Funshine Bear, Friend Bear, Good Luck Bear, Love a Lot, and so forth. Skits, decorations, and devotionals can all be centered around each group's Care Bear. Decorations could include Care Bears, the shapes that are on each of their tummies, white or colorful clouds, castles, blow-up swords, swords cut out of poster board, a mock drawbridge and mote for entering into your campground, and so forth.

Handcart Company

Assign each ward or group a company name: Blacksmith Company, Rescue Aid Company, and so forth. Devotionals could focus on following in the footsteps of the pioneers and Joseph Smith. For the hike, have a mini trek one day at camp; make sure everyone wears long skirts for a real pioneer experience. Have devotionals about individual pioneers who crossed the plains to Utah. Learn about everyday pioneer life and incorporate chores and games into your daily activities, such as a stick pull. Decorations can be anything to do with pioneers: wagons, pioneer memorabilia, rag dolls, butter churns, and so forth. Be sure to make Kick-the-Can Ice Cream sometime during the week.

Joy to the World (A Christmas Camp)

Base the theme on Isaiah 9:6: "For unto us a child is born, unto us a son is given: and the government should be upon his shoulder: and his name shall be called Wonderful, Counsellor, The mighty God, The everlasting Father, The Prince of Peace." The main spiritual focus is to learn about that first Christmas night and why we celebrate it. To successfully acquire the necessary extras for this theme, you will need to plan ahead. Shop the sales in December, before and after Christmas. It will be hard, or practically impossible, to find the little seasonal things last minute. Decorations could include Christmas trees of all sizes; Christmas lights (if you have electricity); stockings; tinsel; garland; wreathes; stars; pinecones; jingle bells; popcorn on a string with cranberries; fake snow; life-size pictures of Santa; pictures of Christ, Mary, and Joseph; a stable; a nativity scene; and so forth—the possibilities are endless. Look through your own Christmas decorations. Ask other leaders to share some of theirs. Be sure to read Christmas stories every day. Sing Christmas hymns and traditional Christmas songs. Be sure to dress in red and green, with Santa hats and bells. Hold a festival of trees where each ward decorates a Christmas tree. Hand out awards for the most creative, most festive, most spiritual, best concept, cutest, funniest, and so forth.

③ Cooking

When you are camping in the great outdoors, it is important that you plan, pack, and prepare food accordingly. Yes, it does take planning and preparation, but it will pay off once you are at camp.

Nutrition

- Well-balanced meals are essential for providing energy and maintaining regular body functions. Make sure the food at camp is nutritious to ensure a happy crowd and a successful week at camp.
- Being outdoors increases our need for water. Plan for at least two quarts of fluids per person each day and more on hike days and hotter days.
- Make sure the menu includes plenty of raw vegetables and fruit.

Planning a Menu

- Plan meals around who you will be feeding. Not everyone will be pleased with every meal, but include a variety so that those with different tastes will still be happy.
- Need menu ideas? Take requests from your young women.
- Consider daily schedules, hikes, allergies, and so forth.
- If there are young women who need to learn certain methods of cooking for certification requirements, remember to plan for those.
- Prepare enough so everyone can have as much as they want. When camping, you need more to eat than you normally would at home.

- Make a *complete* list of ingredients from your menu.
- Look in cookbooks for quantities.
- Make a camp cookbook just for that year. Use a three-ring binder and include step-by-step instructions for each recipe. Be very specific—"Get a bowl and a spoon . . ."—this way you can be sure to bring everything you need to prepare the meal. This also assures that the girls can prepare the meal without you.

Time

- Time needs to be considered when planning a menu. Plan and prepare easier meals on busy days. Save the real time takers for the night the bishopric comes up. Quick and easy meals will make everyone happy.
- Consider prep time, utensils needed, type of fire, and so forth when planning your daily menu.
- Mix puddings, pancake mixes, cake mixes, and salads in ziplock bags so that you can just throw the bag away when you're done to avoid extra dishes to bring and wash. And you can serve pudding in ice cream cones to further cut down on cleanup time.
- Clean up as you go.

Cost

- Shop at warehouse stores (Costco, Sam's Club) for large quantities.
- Watch for sales and buy non-perishables ahead of time.
- Take into consideration what food will last the whole week. Will the bread still be good if you buy it ahead of time?

Preparation

- Do as much preparation as possible at home before going to camp.
- Try out new recipes at home before camp.
- Cook as many items (hamburger, chicken) as possible at home ahead of time with young women. Label and freeze.
- You may want to arrange freezer space with other Young Women leaders or neighbors.
- Freeze as much as possible. It will help keep the coolers colder. Be sure you take items out in plenty of time for them to thaw.
- Grate cheese (or buy pre-grated cheese) beforehand and keep cold.
- Freeze your milk—yes, this can be done. The gallon jug expands a bit while frozen, but it keeps longer and stays cold. Be sure to thaw the day

before it is needed while still keeping it cold. You can usually just leave this gallon of frozen milk out on a table inside of a cabin or tent most of the day to thaw. Once it is mostly thawed, place back in cooler.

- Vegetables like onions, green peppers, celery, green onions, and carrots can be cut up the day before leaving and kept cold at home.
- If rice is on the menu, use Minute Rice. Regular long grain rice takes too much time to cook, especially at higher elevations.
- When making pancakes, use a mix that only requires adding water.
- If chopped tomatoes are needed, use canned. Just drain, and instantly you have nicely chopped tomatoes in the time it takes to open the can. Just don't forget the can opener.
- Label *everything*. Put on each item what day and meal it is for (Tuesday lunch, Wednesday snack).
- When packing food, try to have all the food for each day combined in one or two coolers. This way the food is organized, and you won't have to open every cooler looking for something. This will help keep the food colder for longer.
- Freeze water in one- or two-liter jugs, leaving one to two inches at the top. Use these in place or in addition to ice cubes. As these thaw, they can be used as drinking water.
- Use dry ice on items that need to stay frozen solid. Wrap the dry ice in a paper bag and place on top of the item that needs to stay frozen.
- You may want to store all the bread (without ice) or all the produce (with ice) in a cooler by itself.
- Empty Pringle-type containers make great disposable storage containers for ingredients like flour and sugar.
- It's great to prepare ahead, but make sure to leave enough to do at camp for the girls to certify in the different cooking methods.

Methods

- Be creative in the cooking methods used at camp. You can use the campfire, Dutch ovens, box ovens, reflector ovens, stick cooking, and so forth.
- Be sure to use the right kind of fire for the method of cooking you are using. Write it down as part of the equipment needed for that meal. Be sure to get it started in time to have the proper heat. Start charcoal for Dutch ovens fifteen to twenty minutes before needed.

At Camp

- Plan for lunches that can be prepared without a fire.
- Provide snacks during the day—granola bars, fresh fruit, trail mix, and so forth.
- Keep a cooler of drinks (water or juice) available at all times. This will encourage the girls to drink often. Or keep a five-gallon water cooler full of ice water or punch to provide easy access to drinks. Leave it out on a table with paper cups close by.
- A fun drink to have at camp is homemade root beer. Make it when you first arrive at camp in a five-gallon water cooler. The girls will drink this all week. Toward the end of the week, it starts to turn into slush from the dry ice. This makes a very refreshing treat after a long hike or other activity. It is also a treat for stake visitors or bishopric members to have homemade root beer when they come to visit.
- Make sure the girls and leaders drink lots and lots of water.
- Wash hands often (or use hand sanitizer gel).
- Garbage—have three separate garbage cans at all times: non-burnable, burnable, and recyclable. Burn the burnable garbage daily. Take home the recycle trash and take it to a recycling center. A recycling project could be used as a good works value project in Personal Progress. If extra project hours are needed, you may want to arrange a recycling bin for the entire camp.
- When preparing garbage cans, be sure to use sturdy, heavy-duty plastic or aluminum bins. Make sure there is always a liner in the can before placing anything in it. This will help maintain a clean campground. Always keep a lid on the bin so rodents or small animals can't rummage through it.

Charts

Substitutes

1 (1-oz.) square baking chocolate = 3–4 Tbsp. cocoa + ½ Tbsp. fat
1 Tbsp. cornstarch = 2 Tbsp. flour
1 tsp. baking powder = ¼ tsp. soda + ½ tsp. cream of tartar
1 cup buttermilk = 1 cup milk + 2 Tbsp. vinegar
1 cake compressed yeast = 1 pkg. active dry yeast

Quantities for Large Groups

Food Item	25 people	50 people
rolls	4 dozen	8 dozen
bread	50 slices	100 slices
mayonnaise	1 cup	2–3 cups
mixed fruit	1 quart	2 quarts
cheese	3 lbs.	6 lbs.
soup	1½ gallons	3 gallons
salad dressing	1 pt.	2½ pt.
hamburger	9 lbs.	18 lbs.
chicken	13 lbs.	25–35 lbs.
mashed potatoes	9 lbs.	20 lbs.
tuna mixed with mayo	1½ quarts	2½–3 quarts
Jell-O salad	¾ gallon	1¼ gallons
canned vegetables	12–13 cups	25–30 cups
lettuce (for salads)	4 heads	8 heads
lemonade	2 gallons	4 gallons

Equivalency Chart

3 tsp. = 1 Tbsp.
4 Tbsp. = ¼ cup
8 Tbsp. = ½ cup
16 Tbsp. = 1 cup
5 Tbsp. + 1 tsp. = ⅓ cup
4 oz. = ½ cup
8 oz. = 1 cup
16 oz. = 1 lb.
2 cups = 1 pt.
2 pt. = 1 qt.
1 qt. = 4 cups
1 cup cream = 2 cups whipped
1 lb. shredded cheese = 4 cups

1 lemon = 3 Tbsp. juice
1 orange = ⅓ cup juice
2 cups sugar = 1 lb.
3½–4 cups powdered sugar = 1 lb.
4 cups flour = 1 lb.
4 slices bread = 1 cup crumbs
14 square graham crackers = 1 cup crumbs
3 medium bananas = 1 cup mashed
3 cups dry corn flakes = 1 cup crushed
10 miniature marshmallows = 1 large marshmallow

Menu Ideas

When planning a menu, keep in mind that there are several meals that can be served for both lunch and dinner. Plan meals that are easy to prepare. You will enjoy your camping experience so much more if you are not continually cooking over a fire.

Breakfast

cold cereal	muffins	eggs and bacon (or sausage)
fresh fruit	scones	egg mcmuffins
yogurt	orange rolls	hash browns or fried potatoes
granola bars	English muffins	breakfast casserole
bagels	cinnamon rolls	breakfast in a bag
French toast	pancakes	mountain man breakfast

Lunch

sack lunch	potato bar	Hawaiian hay stacks
hoagies	taco salad	soup in bread bowls
hot dogs	chef salad	tuna sandwiches
PBJ sandwiches	sloppy joes	chicken salad sandwiches
bagel sandwiches	hamburgers	egg salad sandwiches

Dinner

hot dogs	Caesar salad	sweet and sour chicken
potato bar	turkey in a pit	barbecue cups
Navajo tacos	tin foil dinners	Dutch oven chicken or ribs

Dutch Oven Cooking

Below are the basic first steps in preparing and using a Dutch oven.

- To season a Dutch oven at home: wash your Dutch oven with mild soapy water, rinse thoroughly, and dry. Using a cotton cloth, rub all surfaces with vegetable oil. Add enough oil to cover the inside bottom of the Dutch oven. Place in preheated oven at 350 degrees for thirty minutes. Remove from oven and carefully circulate the oil to cover all the sides and bottom. Add more oil and heat at 200 degrees for one hour. Turn oven off and leave in overnight. In the morning, rub all surfaces with the remaining oil and remove excess.
- If your Dutch oven rusts, discolors, or has a metallic taste, this is a sign that your seasoning has been removed. Follow above directions to re-season.
- When you store your Dutch oven, put a paper towel inside to absorb moisture. Keep lid on in storage. Store in a dry place.
- When using charcoal briquettes, place the correct number of coals on the top and bottom. Place them in a checkerboard pattern. When it states to put coals on the bottom of your Dutch oven, simply place the coals on the ground, then place the oven on top of them. Look for Dutch ovens that have legs.

Size of Oven	Top	Bottom
8-inch	6–8	4–6
10-inch	8–10	6–8
12-inch	10–12	8–10
14-inch	12–16	10–12
16-inch	16–18	12–16

- For heat control: One white briquette equals forty degrees (example: 10 white briquettes = 400 degrees). Because charcoal briquettes give off a great deal of heat, check food periodically to make sure you have good heat control.
- The cooking time is approximate. It depends on your altitude and the item you are cooking (potatoes take longer than chicken breasts, etc.). It usually takes as much time to cook something in a Dutch oven as it does to cook something at home.
- Don't skimp on the charcoal. (When a recipe says *coals*, it means charcoal briquettes.) Buy a name brand charcoal. Store brands usually

run out of heat faster, thus needing more coals to replace the burned-out ones.

- When using coals straight from the fire, cover the bottom and top of Dutch oven well. Heat from the coals of a fire are a little harder to control than heat from briquettes. When using fire coals, check often to be sure your food is cooking properly and at the right speed.
- For easier cleanup, always line your Dutch oven with foil. Fold the foil down at the top so the lid will still fit securely. Spray foil with non-stick cooking spray.
- Your Dutch oven should be burned out to clean. Remove all particles of food; place on a heat source (back on the coals or in a fire), burn remaining food inside to ash, scrape sides and bottom, then remove all particles with a slightly damp rag. Grease all surfaces with vegetable oil before storing, including the bottom of the oven and the top and bottom of the lid. You may also clean it out with very mild soap and water. Be sure to oil again when clean.

Dutch Oven Recipes

German Pancakes

2 cups milk
1 dozen eggs
2 cups flour
1 stick butter

Combine milk, eggs, and flour until smooth. Set aside. Melt butter in 14-inch Dutch oven over 10 hot coals. Pour batter over butter. Cover. Cook with 20 coals on top and 10 on bottom for 20 minutes. The batter may rise up and lift the lid. Serve with fruit pie filling or with hot maple syrup and powdered sugar.

Eggs

To cook eggs in a Dutch oven, simply turn the lid upside down on the coals and cook on the lid as a griddle. Bacon or french toast can also be cooked this way. You can also cook them inside of the Dutch oven.

Mountain Man Breakfast

1 lb. bacon or pre-cooked sausage
1 small onion, chopped
1 (2-lb.) pkg. hash browns
1 dozen eggs
½ lb. grated cheddar cheese

Cut bacon into small pieces. Cook bacon and onion in 12-inch Dutch oven over 8 coals. Stir in hash browns. Cover and place 12 coals on top. Brown and heat through about 10 minutes, stirring occasionally. Mix eggs together. Pour over browned hash browns. Cover and cook until eggs are done, 10–15 minutes, with coals on top and bottom. Sprinkle with cheese. Cover until cheese is melted, about 5 minutes.

Breakfast Casserole

8 slices of bread, cubed
2 lbs. cooked sausage
2 cups grated cheddar cheese
1 dozen eggs, whipped by hand
4 cups milk

Line 12-inch Dutch oven with foil. Spray with non-stick cooking spray. Put bread in oven, crumble sausage over bread, then sprinkle with cheese. Mix together eggs and milk. Pour into oven. Bake for 35–40 minutes with 10 coals on bottom and 12 coals on top. Check occasionally. Adjust heat as needed. Feeds a crowd.

Scones

oil
frozen scone dough, thawed

Heat oil in a Dutch oven over hot coals (charcoal briquettes or coals from the fire pit). Break off pieces of dough and flatten into a circle. Cook in hot oil. Turn once. Serve with honey butter or powdered sugar.

Vegetable Medley

2 cups fresh broccoli
2 cups fresh cauliflower

1 onion, chopped
5 mushrooms, sliced
1 cup water
seasoned salt and pepper
butter
1–1½ cups grated cheddar cheese

Mix vegetables together. Place in Dutch oven. Pour water over top. Season with seasoned salt and pepper. Add several pats of butter to top. Cover. Cook with 10–12 coals on top and bottom. Steam until done. Check often to monitor water and doneness. Add more water if needed (do not add too much). When vegetables are done, drain off leftover water. Spread cheddar cheese over top. Cover and cook until cheese is melted.

Dutch Oven Ribs

12–14 boneless beef ribs
2 bottles barbecue sauce

Line 12- or 14-inch Dutch oven with foil. Spray with non-stick cooking spray. Place ribs in oven. Pour on barbecue sauce. Cook with 12–14 coals on top and 10–12 on bottom for 1–1½ hours. Check after 45 minutes. Adjust heat if necessary.

Dutch Oven Potatoes

1 lb. bacon, cut into small pieces
12–15 potatoes, thinly sliced (with or without peel)
2–3 onions, diced
salt and pepper to taste
pats of butter
¼ cup water
1 can cream of mushroom soup
3 cups grated cheddar cheese

Place 12- or 14-inch Dutch oven over 10–12 coals. Fry bacon until crisp and remove from Dutch oven. Layer ½ of the potato slices, onion, bacon, seasonings, and butter pats. Repeat. Add water to provide moisture. Cover and cook with 10 coals on bottom and 12 on top until potatoes are tender, 35–45 minutes. When ¾ of the way done, stir in soup. When done, add cheese to top and cook just until cheese is melted. Serves 10.

Prepare ahead tip: You can cook the bacon ahead of time and keep cold until ready to use.

Dutch Oven Chicken

12 chicken breasts
2 bottles barbecue sauce *or* 3 cans cream of chicken soup and 1 can water

Line 12- or 14-inch Dutch oven with aluminum foil. Spray with non-stick cooking spray. Place chicken in Dutch oven. Pour sauce over chicken. Cook with 12–14 coals on the bottom and 10–12 coals on top. Adjust according to cooking speed. Cook for about 1 hour. Serves 12.

Sweet and Sour Chicken

oil
½ cup flour
½ cup cornstarch
3 lbs. chicken breasts (each cut in half)
2 eggs, beaten
garlic salt

Sauce
1 cup water
¼ tsp. salt
¾ cup sugar
1 tsp. chicken bouillon crystals *or* 1 bouillon cube
½ cup ketchup
1 Tbsp. soy sauce

Heat oil in 12- or 14-inch Dutch oven. Mix flour and cornstarch together in a large ziplock bag. Dip chicken in beaten egg, then shake in bag of flour mixture. Brown chicken in hot oil, and sprinkle with garlic salt. Remove from Dutch oven. Drain off excess oil. You may just want to soak up the oil with a paper towel. Don't wipe dry.

Mix together sauce ingredients and pour into Dutch oven. You may want to double the sauce recipe. Bring to a boil. Add browned chicken. Cover. Bake for 1 hour using 12–16 coals on top and 10–12 coals on bottom. Turn halfway through baking time. Serve with rice.

Prepare ahead tip: At home, prepare as recipe states. Instead of placing browned chicken in Dutch oven, place in a large ziplock bag. Pour sauce over chicken. Freeze. When ready to cook, slide partially thawed meat and sauce mixture out of plastic bag into a Dutch oven and cook as directed.

Monkey Bread

1½ cup melted butter, divided
Italian seasoning to taste
4 cans refrigerator rolls

Melt ½ cup butter in 12-inch Dutch oven. In a ziplock bag, mix 1 cup melted butter and Italian seasoning. Cut each biscuit into fourths. Place a few pieces at a time in bag to coat with butter and seasoning. Place in Dutch oven. Cover. Bake for 30–40 minutes, checking after 20 minutes, with 12 coals on top and 6 on bottom.

You can substitute the Italian seasoning with garlic powder or cinnamon-sugar. When using cinnamon-sugar, add ¼ cup evaporated milk, 1 cup sugar, and 2 teaspoons cinnamon with melted butter on bottom of Dutch oven. Invert onto a plate when done cooking.

Pineapple Upside-Down Cake

2 Tbsp. butter
1 (16-oz.) can pineapple slices
½ cup brown sugar
1 yellow cake mix
ingredients needed according to cake mix package instructions

Preheat coals. Line Dutch oven with aluminum foil. Melt butter in bottom of oven over coals. Drain fruit, reserving juice. Arrange pineapple on top of butter. Sprinkle with brown sugar and 3 tablespoons pineapple juice. Prepare cake mix according to package directions. Pour over fruit. Cover with lid. Cook with 10–12 coals on both top and bottom for 35–40 minutes. Serves 12–14.

Apple Crisp

2 cups brown sugar
2 cups flour

1 cup rolled oats
1 cup butter, softened
2 cans sliced apples
cinnamon

Mix together brown sugar, flour, and rolled oats. Cut in butter so mix is crumbly. Set aside. Pour apples into prepared 12- or 14-inch Dutch oven (lined with foil, sprayed). Sprinkle with cinnamon. Spread on crumbly topping. Cover. Bake with 10–12 coals on top and 8–10 coals on bottom for 20–30 minutes.

Cinnamon-Sugar Donuts

cooking oil
refrigerator rolls
cinnamon-sugar

Pour oil 1½ inches deep in Dutch oven. Preheat oil over coals, not flames, but be careful not to over heat. Make a hole in the rolls to form a donut shape. Drop each donut from a spoon into the hot oil. Turn once. Remove from oil and roll in cinnamon-sugar.

Hot Fudge Pudding Cake

2 cups flour
1½ cups sugar
½ cup + 4 Tbsp. cocoa, divided
4 tsp. baking powder
½ tsp. salt
1 cup milk
4 Tbsp. oil
2 cups chopped nuts
2 cups brown sugar
3½ cups hot water

Prepare a 12-inch Dutch oven by lining with foil and spraying with non-stick cooking spray. Mix flour, sugar, 4 tablespoons cocoa, baking powder, and salt in a bowl. Blend in milk and oil; stir in nuts. Pour into Dutch oven. Stir together brown sugar and remaining ½ cup cocoa and sprinkle over batter. Pour hot water over batter. Bake for 45–55 minutes. Serve hot and spoon sauce over each serving. Serve with whipped cream or ice cream.

Soda Pop Cobbler (Lazy-Man Cobbler)

1 large can fruit, drained, or pie filling
1 yellow cake mix
1 can lemon-lime soda

Prepare a 12 inch Dutch oven by lining with foil and spraying with non-stick cooking spray. Spread fruit or pie filling (apple, cherry, peach, or pineapple) evenly over bottom of oven. Sprinkle with dry cake mix. Pour soda over cake mix. Do not stir. Cover with lid. Bake for 30 minutes with 10–12 coals on bottom and 8–10 coals on top. Adjust heat if necessary.

Fancy Peach Cobbler

Crust
1½ cups flour
2 tsp. baking powder
1 large pkg. vanilla pudding, dry
3 Tbsp. powdered milk, dry
2 eggs
1 cup water
6 Tbsp. butter, softened

Filling
1–2 quarts fruit (peaches or cherry pie filling)

Topping
2 (8-oz.) pkgs. cream cheese, softened
1 cup sugar
6 generous Tbsp. fruit juice

Prepare a 12-inch Dutch oven by lining with foil and spraying with non-stick cooking spray. Combine dry crust ingredients. Mix together eggs, water, and softened butter and add to dry ingredients. Beat 2 minutes and pour into prepared oven. Spread filling on top of crust, not quite to edges. Mix topping ingredients together and place on top of fruit, leaving ½ inch on all sides. Garnish by sprinkling with cinnamon-sugar. Bake 30–35 minutes with 10–12 coals on top and 8–10 on bottom.

Peach or Cherry Cobbler

2 small cans peaches *or* 1 large can cherry pie filling
1 yellow cake mix
ingredients needed according to cake mix instructions

Preheat coals. Prepare a 12-inch Dutch oven by lining with foil and spraying with non-stick cooking spray. Spread fruit into oven (drain peaches, leaving only a little juice). Prepare cake batter according to package directions. Pour over fruit and cover with lid. Bake with 10–12 coals on bottom and 8–10 coals on top for 30–45 minutes. Serves 10–14. Serve with Kick-the-Can Ice Cream (recipe below) or whipped topping. Make only 1 batch per Dutch oven.

Kick-the-Can Ice Cream

1 cup milk
1 cup whipping cream
½ cup sugar
½ tsp. vanilla
1 egg (optional)
nuts or fruit as desired

Mix all ingredients together and place in a tin can. Cover and secure lid with tape. Place tin can in a larger tin can (coffee can, #10). Pack with ice and rock salt. Cover with tight lid and secure with tape. Roll can for 10 minutes. Open cans and stir. Replace ice and rock salt and roll for another 10 minutes. It's fun to have two people rolling to each other. This recipe is good with any cobbler recipe or alone. It goes right along with a pioneer theme too.

This can also be done in ziplock freezer bags. Use quart-size bag to hold ingredients and gallon-size to hold ice and salt. Pass from person to person, squeezing and shaking.

Campfire Recipes

Orange Muffins

muffin mix
ingredients needed according to muffin mix package
oranges

Make muffin batter according to package directions. Cut an orange in half (down the middle, not from end to end). Hollow out ends, removing orange from peel and leaving peel whole. Fill one side of orange peel almost full of muffin batter, place other half of the orange on top (so it resembles a whole orange). Wrap in heavy aluminum foil. Place on hot coals (not flames) for 10–15 minutes. When done, open up orange and eat muffin.

Breakfast in a Bag

2 strips bacon
2 eggs
small paper sack
roasting stick

Rub the strips of bacon on the bottom of the paper sack. Lay bacon on bottom of sack. Crack eggs and drop on top of bacon. Fold paper bag down three times. Poke a roasting stick through the folds. Suspend over hot coals or a fire. Cook until eggs are done. As long as the paper bag does not come in direct contact with a flame or coals, it will not burn.

Turkey in a Pit

1. Clean and wash an average-sized turkey as you usually would (remove the neck, insides, and so forth).
2. Wrap the entire turkey in two layers of aluminum foil.
3. Cover the foil with a damp burlap bag (old potato bag). This will act as a steamer.
4. Wrap with another 2 layers of foil.
5. Wrap the entire outside of the turkey with wire and make a handle at the end so it can be pulled to the top when finished. Place the handle so that the turkey can rest upside down.
6. Dig a pit that will be 3 times as deep and 2 times as wide, when lined with rocks, as the turkey. Line the entire inside of the pit with flat rocks all the way to the top. This is what will eventually cook the turkey.
7. Begin a fire in the pit that will burn hard and hot for 4–5 hours. When the time is up and the fire has burned itself out, remove ¼ of the coals.
8. Place the turkey in prepared pit and cover with the remaining coals. Cover the entire pit back up with the loose dirt, leaving only the wire handle sticking up.
9. Allow to cook for 24–26 hours.

Baked Potatoes

potatoes
desired toppings (butter, sour cream, broccoli and cheese, chili, onions)

Wash and clean potatoes. Wrap in a layer of heavy-duty aluminum foil. Cook on hot coals for 30–45 minutes. Check after 20 minutes. Potatoes are done when they are soft when squeezed. Top with your favorite toppings.

Tin Foil Dinner

1 chicken breast *or* ¼ lb. hamburger
potatoes *or* frozen tater tots
desired vegetables (carrots, zucchini, squash, tomato)
onion
cream of chicken soup or cream of mushroom soup
seasonings

On 2 large, greased pieces of foil, layer meat, potatoes, vegetables, onion, soup, and seasonings. Fold ends of foil up to middle, rolling down to seal. Cook with hot coals on top and bottom for 30–45 minutes, turning every 15–20 minutes. Check after 20 minutes and adjust heat if needed.

Prepare ahead tip: You can cook the meat and vegetables before assembling, then when ready to cook, simply heat it up for about 20 minutes.

Chocolate Bananas

1 banana
2 Tbsp. milk chocolate chips
2 Tbsp. mini marshmallows

Cut a slice down the length of the peel, cutting through to fruit. Fill slice with chocolate chips and marshmallows. Wrap tightly with foil. Cook for 5 minutes over coals.

Campfire Fudge

3½ cups powdered sugar
½ cup cocoa
1 cup butter, softened

3 oz. cream cheese, softened
1 tsp. vanilla

Place dry ingredients in a large ziplock bag. When ready to use, add butter, cream cheese, and vanilla. Pass from person to person around the campfire until well mixed. Add nuts and marshmallows just before serving.

Roasted Starbursts

Starburst candies
roasting sticks

Unwrap candy. Poke 1 onto a stick. Roast over hot coals until outside starts to bubble. Let cool for about 30 seconds. Watch out: these can burn tongues. They should have a crunchy outside and a soft, gooey inside.

Cinnamon Biscuits on a Stick

3 cans refrigerator rolls
½ cup (or more) butter, melted
1 cup sugar, mixed with cinnamon, to taste—in a ziplock bag

Wrap 1 biscuit around the end of a roasting stick or a willow. Wrap it so it resembles a snake. Pinch the ends together to hold it onto the stick. Roast over hot coals until browned and no longer doughy inside, 5–15 minutes. Remove from stick and dip in melted butter until covered. Cover with cinnamon-sugar. Eat and enjoy!

S'mores with a Twist

marshmallows
chocolate graham crackers

Roast marshmallows over hot coals. Place in between 2 chocolate graham cracker squares.

Homemade Hot Chocolate

3 cups dry powdered milk
1½ cups powdered sugar
1½ cups chocolate milk drink mix
2 cups non-dairy creamer

Mix all ingredients together. Place ⅓ cup mix in each mug; add hot water and stir. Place water in a big pot over your dinner fire. When your evening campfire is through, your water will be ready for hot chocolate.

Simple Recipes

These are recipes that need no heat or only a campfire or propane stove. These can be partially prepared at home, making the evening meal much simpler.

Chef Salad

3 lbs. salad mix
2 cups cubed ham
2 cups cubed turkey breast
2 cups cubed chicken
2 cups cubed cheddar cheese
2 cups cubed Provolone or Swiss cheese
2 cups chopped celery
2 cups chopped cucumbers
2 bunches green onions, chopped
diced tomatoes
salad dressing

Mix all ingredients together. Serve from one big bowl. Serves 20–25.

Sloppy Joes

hamburger
sloppy joe seasoning mix
ingredients according to seasoning package instructions
hamburger buns

Brown hamburger and add seasoning mix according to package directions. Cool. Place in a freezer bag and place in freezer. Remove from freezer and allow to thaw before cooking. When ready to prepare meal, remove seasoned meat from bag and heat through.

Taco Salad

taco seasoning
hamburger
salad mix
grated cheese
chopped tomatoes (canned)
olives
chili or chili beans (canned, with juice)
chopped onions
Doritos
Ranch or Thousand Island dressing

Add taco seasoning to hamburger and cook until browned. Freeze in freezer bags. When ready to prepare meal, heat up meat. Mix with remaining ingredients.

Six pounds of seasoned hamburger will make a salad big enough to serve 25–30 people.

Hawaiian Hay Stacks

5 cans cream of chicken soup
2½ cups chicken broth
5 cups cooked, cubed chicken
20 cups cooked rice
3 bunches green onions, chopped
2 (20-oz.) cans pineapple tidbits
1–2 cans tomatoes, chopped
1 small pkg. frozen peas
1 bag chow mein noodles
2½ cups grated cheese
1 stalk celery, chopped
1 small bag slivered almonds
1½ cups chopped green pepper
1 bag coconut

Combine soup, broth, and chicken. Heat through. To serve, place some rice on plate and layer on remaining ingredients according to taste. Serve 20–25.

No Bake Cookies

2 cups sugar
½ cup milk
½ cup butter
⅛ tsp. salt
3 Tbsp. cocoa
1 tsp. vanilla
1 cup peanut butter
3 cups rolled oats

Combine sugar, milk, butter, salt, and cocoa in a large saucepan. Bring to full boil. Boil for 1 minute. Remove from heat. Add vanilla and peanut butter. Stir until smooth. Add rolled oats and mix. Drop by tablespoonfuls onto waxed paper. Let cool. Makes 4 dozen.

Navajo Tacos

3 cups flour
3 tsp. baking powder
½ tsp. salt
1½ cup milk
hamburger
onions
cheese
tomatoes

Stir together dry ingredients. Add milk and stir. Divide dough into 6–8 pieces. Roll or pat each until ¼-inch thick. Fry in hot oil, till browned on both sides. Top with your favorite taco fillings: hamburger, onions, cheese, tomatoes, and so forth.

Prepare ahead tip: Brown one pound hamburger. Add taco seasoning according to package directions. Freeze. Thaw and heat before using.

Box Oven Cooking

Cooking with a box oven can be a very rewarding experience. The aroma of baking food will stream throughout the camp, inviting everybody to come and have a taste. Box oven cooking is an easy way to cook while camping.

How to Make a Box Oven

You will need the following supplies to make your own box oven:

1–2 apple box lids (you can get these at your local grocery store)
aluminum foil
duct tape
4 identically-sized empty vegetable cans, label removed

Take the apple box lid(s) and cover the inside and outside completely with foil, taping down occasionally to hold foil in place. Make sure that you don't have too much tape exposed on the inside of the lid. Curl tape under seams. If the tape is exposed, it will eventually get too hot and fall off. Use as much tape on the outside as needed.

How to Cook in a Box Oven

You can bake almost anything in a box oven. The cooking times may differ in the altitude of the mountains, but other than that, have fun and experiment. If the item you are baking takes longer than twenty or thirty minutes, you'll want to have two sets of coals, one ready to cook on and one ready to change when the first batch dies out.

Make sure that the baking dish you plan on using (9x13, 8-inch square, cookie sheet, pie pan) fits under the apple box lid you have prepared. The lid needs to cover the dish completely and touch the ground on all four sides.

1. Start coals. They are ready when they turn white, or mostly white. Each white briquette contributes forty degrees to the cooking temperature. So for a 400-degree oven, you would need ten white briquettes.
2. When coals are ready, arrange them on a piece of foil in a checker-board pattern so they will all fit underneath your cooking pan.
3. Place the four empty vegetable cans, standing upright, around coals. These are what hold up your baking dish.
4. Place baking dish on top of cans, each can on a corner of the dish, so that the baking pan is elevated above the coals.
5. Cover with prepared apple box lid. Prop up one corner of the lid with a small rock for air circulation.
6. Cook according to recipe. You may need to cook some things slightly longer than the recipe calls for. Check food while cooking and adjust time accordingly.

7. Make sure you cook on flat ground. If it is not flat, you will have sloping cakes, cookies, pies, and so forth.

Box Oven Recipes

Cowboy Cookies

1 cup shortening
1 cup brown sugar
1 cup white sugar
2 eggs
1 tsp. vanilla
1 tsp. soda
½ tsp. baking powder
½ tsp. salt
2 cups flour
1½ cups rolled oats
1 pkg. chocolate chips

Mix all ingredients together. Drop on cookie sheet by rounded teaspoon. Bake in a 350-degree oven for 12 minutes or until done. Makes 4 dozen cookies.

Coconut Oatmeal Cookies

1 cup flour
½ tsp. baking powder
½ tsp. salt
½ tsp. baking soda
½ cup shortening
½ cup sugar
½ cup brown sugar
1 egg
1 tsp. vanilla
½ cup rolled oats
1 cup coconut

Stir together flour, baking powder, salt, and baking soda; set aside. Cream shortening with sugars. Add egg and vanilla; beat well. Add flour mixture gradually and mix until smooth. Stir in rolled oats and coconut. Drop by rounded teaspoons onto ungreased cookie sheet. Bake in a 375-degree oven for 9–12 minutes. Makes 3 dozen cookies.

Brownies

1½ cup flour
2/3 cup cocoa
2 cups sugar
1 cup butter, melted
4 eggs
2 tsp. vanilla

Mix together flour, cocoa, and sugar. Add melted butter, eggs, and vanilla. Pour into a greased 9x13 pan. Bake in a 350-degree oven for 30 minutes.

Cake Mix Cookies

1 cake mix (any flavor)
1½ cups water
2 eggs
2 Tbsp. shortening
1½–2 cups flour
frosting

Combine ingredients except frosting as you would a cake. Bake on an ungreased cookie sheet in a 350-degree oven for 6–8 minutes. Frost.

Barbecue Cups

1 lb. hamburger
½ cup chopped onion
¼ cup ketchup or to taste
½ cup barbecue sauce
2 pkgs. refrigerator rolls
½–¾ cup grated cheddar cheese

Brown hamburger and onion. Add ketchup and barbecue sauce. Place roll dough in each space of a muffin tin, pushing dough up the sides to form a cup. Place browned meat mixture into cups. Sprinkle with cheese. Bake in a 350-degree oven for 10 minutes or until rolls are done. Makes 20 cups, 6 servings.

Prepare ahead tip: Brown hamburger and onion; add ketchup and barbecue sauce. Place in a ziplock freezer bag. Freeze. When ready to prepare meal, thaw out meat and heat in a small pan on a fire or propane stove. Place in cups and bake.

Bread

1 loaf Rhodes frozen dough

Allow to thaw and rise in bread pan. Cook in oven according to directions on package.

Sweet Corn Bread

½ cup melted butter
1 cup sugar
2 eggs
1½ cups flour
2 tsp. baking powder
1 cup cornmeal
½ tsp. salt
1½ cups milk

Mix all ingredients. Batter will be runny. Bake in a 9x13 pan in a 375-degree oven for 25–30 minutes. This can also be cooked in a Dutch oven. Just pour batter into oven, cover, and cook with 12–14 coals on top and 10–12 coals on bottom.

Pretzels

1 Tbsp. yeast
½ cup warm water
1 tsp. honey
1 tsp. salt
1⅓ cup flour
1 beaten egg

Dissolve yeast in water. Add honey, salt, and flour. Knead 3–4 minutes. Roll pieces out and form into letters or pretzel shapes. Brush with beaten egg. Sprinkle with additional salt. Bake on a cookie sheet in a 425-degree oven for 6–7 minutes.

(4) Certification

Certification is one of the key purposes of Girls Camp. As stated in the *Young Women Camp Manual*, "With the world of nature as your classroom, you can experience the wonder of God's creations and learn skills that will help you become self-reliant and able to live comfortably in the outdoors" (page 7).

Certification at a Glance

Through certification, the young women are accomplishing all of the purposes and goals of Girls Camp:

- Draw closer to Heavenly Father and his Son, Jesus Christ.
- Feel the influence of the Spirit.
- Serve others.
- Build friendships and unity.
- Learn skills.
- Appreciate God's creations.
- Have fun!

The tables on the next two pages are a breakdown of what each certification year needs to learn at camp. These provide a quick, one-glance look at what you need to teach to your young women.

	Spiritual	Environment and Safety	Hiking	First Aid
1st Year	• Study scriptures 15 min. a day. Read Moses 2:1–31 and Genesis 1:1–31 and share thoughts.	• Sanitation; hiking and camp garbage disposal. • Fire regulations; properly extinguish fire. • Store and prepare food properly. * Recycle.	• Plan and participate in a 3-mile hike. • Explain what to do if you get lost.	• Learn first 4 steps. • Heimlich maneuver. • Learn how to treat poisoning and excessive bleeding. • Fold and use a cravat bandage. • First-aid kit
2nd Year	• Study scriptures 15 min. a day. Read JS—H 1:1–20 and record thoughts.	• Demonstrate two methods of purifying drinking water.	• Plan and participate in a 5-mile hike. • Learn how to signal for help.	• Learn treatment for shock, heat stroke, heat exhaustion, fainting, hypothermia, and frostbite. • Show rescue breathing.
3rd Year	• Study scriptures 15 min. a day. Read Mosiah 18:1–17 and record thoughts.	• Learn to extinguish accidental fires. • Safe drinking water; ways to purify. * Waterfront and hiking safety.	• Participate in an organized hike. • Use a compass in an orienteering activity.	• Learn about stings, burns, blisters, and insect and snake bites. • Demonstrate CPR.
4th Year	• Study scriptures 15 min. a day. • Read Matthew 26:36–46; D&C 88:42–44; Moses 1:37–39; and D&C 67:2 and record thoughts.	• Demonstrate and teach ways to protect the environment. • Carry out a project.	* Plan and participate in a backpacking trip.	• Signs of broken bones; treatment. • 4 ways to transport victim. • Review and demonstrate first aid skills from levels 1–3.

	Service	Nature	Skills	Other Activities
1st Year	• Participate in camp chores. • Serve others.	• Thank Heavenly Father for his creations. * Identify 6 plants and 3 animals. * 30 min. observation.	• Cook at least 2 items. * Tie a square knot, 2 half hitches, and a bowline and know their uses.	• Plan and present a song or a skit.
2nd Year	• Participate in camp chores. • Serve others.	• Identify cloud formations. * 30 minutes observation and prayer. * Learn poisonous vs. edible plants.	• Good nutrition; plan and prepare meal. • Find direction by sun and stars. * 2 kinds of fires * Knife safety and care.	• Plan and participate in a flag-raising ceremony or devotional.
3rd Year	• Help fill a need; complete assignments. * Help a younger or disabled camper fulfill the certification requirements.	• Observe nature. • Express your feelings in an art form and share it.	• Start a fire without matches; make waterproof matches. * Make 3 types of emergency shelters. * Try 2 different types of outdoor cooking.	• Teach a song or game.
4th Year	• Identify a need and plan to fulfill the need. * Disability project.	• Study night sky and read scriptures. • Weather safety. • Plan and participate in a nature walk or hike. * Teach something about nature to a group.	• Prepare meals using 2 different methods. * Demonstrate how to make a bedroll and emergency ground bed.	• Get-to-know-you game. • Plan a skit, song, or scripture story.

* Optional

First Aid Requirements

The Race for Life is a fun, educational activity to do when teaching a group of young women first aid. It is basically a mock disaster of injuries. You will need to do a different injury for each level of certification. This is good to do on a ward or stake level because it will teach all the girls some of their required certification at one activity.

The first thing that needs to be done is to have a class on each of the first aid certification requirements. This should be done a week or two before the scheduled "disaster." Teach the young woman about each injury. Help them feel confident with first aid and how to administer it. Knowledge is the key to a successful first aid certification.

Below is an overview of the first aid certification requirements. Those marked with an asterisk work well for the Race for Life.

1st Year	• Purpose of first aid and first four steps of first aid
	• Heimlich maneuver
	* First aid for excessive bleeding, poisoning
	* Fold and use a cravat bandage
	• First-aid kit
2nd Year	* Treat shock, heat stroke, heat exhaustion, fainting, hypothermia, frostbite
	• Show rescue breathing
3rd Year	* Insect bites, stings, burns, blisters, snakebites
	• Demonstrate CPR
4th Year	* Learn the signs of a broken bone; treatment
	* Learn and demonstrate four ways to transport a victim
	• Review and demonstrate first aid skills from levels 1–3

Note: Practice CPR and rescue breathing should *not* be performed on a person. This should be done separately with a mannequin specifically designed for CPR training. The Heimlich maneuver should be done with caution.

You'll need the following equipment: stage or Halloween makeup; a broken chicken bone to look like a real bone; book from your local library about stage makeup techniques; triangular bandages or bandanas; items to make a splint (padding, branch or stick, strips of cloth); first-aid items necessary to administer first aid to the "victim."

It is easiest to do the Race for Life outdoors, preferably in the wilderness. But you can also do it in a backyard, park, church parking lot, or church cultural hall. Have your YCLs make each other up according to the injury they will be portraying. Make these injuries as convincing as possible. Don't be afraid to really play them up with lots of fake blood; a nice gash on the head is going to bleed, so make sure it does!

When dealing with queasy or easily disturbed young women, use caution when arriving upon the injured person. You may want to take them aside and warn them of what is to come.

Divide the young women into groups by certification level. It is best to have no more than six to eight girls in each group. We want everyone to have a part in helping their injured friend. Place each "injured" YCL in a designated spot. Have the girls find her, assess the situation, administer first aid, then transport her back to the central location. Have a leader with each group to gently guide the young women if they don't remember what needs to be done next.

At the end of the activity, hand out awards to each group for their hard work. You may want to make a shrinky dink for their camp necklaces—a heart with a bandage on it.

Flag Certification

As part of the certifying process, second years need to learn the basics of raising and lowering a flag and how to do it reverently and with respect. Properly retiring a worn, ripped, or old flag can be a very spiritual, uplifting experience for the young women. Don't retire a flag every year; it seems to lose its significance if done too frequently.

This outline can be changed according to the number of girls that will be there. Assign speaking parts accordingly. You may choose any patriotic songs you wish. Be sure to make this a patriotic ceremony.

Preparation

1. Obtain a flag that is worn, ripped, or old and needs to be properly retired. You may want to check your local Boy Scout troop, post office, schools, friends, and so forth.
2. Find out some details about the flag (these will be told as part of the ceremony): when it was first raised, where it has flown, how long

it has flown at that location, if it has ever flown at half mast, any memorable events or facts.

3. Make a bed of coals the size of the flag (or pieces of flag). Make sure the coals are hot enough to burn the flag completely.

4. Prepare your young women for what is about to take place. Emphasize that burning a flag, when done properly, is not disrespectful.

Ceremony

Begin the ceremony with a regular opening exercises.

Conducting:
Opening Song: "This Land is Your Land"
Opening Prayer:
Song: "God Bless the USA" (sung by all YCLs)
Meaning of the Stars and Stripes: YCLs

YCL 1 The U.S. flag is more than just some brightly colored cloth. It is a symbol of our nation. Seven red stripes and six white stripes—together they represent the original thirteen colonies that gained us liberty.

YCL 2 The red stripes remind us of the lifeblood of brave men and women who were ready to die for this, their country. The white stripes remind us of purity and cleanliness of purpose, thought, word, and deed.

YCL 3 The blue is for truth and justice, like the eternal blue of the star-filled heavens. The stars represent the fifty sovereign states of our union.

YCL 4 The U.S. flag should be treated with respect when it's flying, and it should be treated with respect when it's retired. The American's Creed states, "It is my duty to my Country to love it, to respect its Constitution, to obey its laws, to respect its flag, and to defend it against all enemies."

YCL 5 Therefore, we retire flags with dignity and respect when they become worn, torn, faded, or badly soiled.

YCL 6   This flag is ready to be retired. Its history is as follows:
First raised (when):
At (location):
Memorable events or facts:

Leaders   Two leaders will cut the flag. After it is cut, proceed.

YCL 7   A flag ceases to be a flag when it is cut into pieces. We cut the flag into four pieces: three red and white striped banners and the blue star field. We leave the blue field intact because no one should ever let the union be broken.

YCL 8   As the parts of the flag are placed in the fire. Remember, old flags never die; they just get fired up!

It is helpful to cut up the flag so as many as possible can have the opportunity to participate in the flag retirement. Cut the flag into four pieces by cutting once lengthwise along the edge of the star field and once by width along the other edge of the star field.

If you choose to cut the flag, assign girls into groups of three or four, each with a YCL to help. On each piece of flag, tie a four-foot piece of twine to each corner by bunching up the end and tying a knot with rope. This will provide a place for the girls to hold the rope instead of the piece of flag, preventing possible burns from the fire. Each group then places one piece of flag carefully into the fire.

While the flag is burning, have everyone sing "The Star Spangled Banner." Remain standing and quiet until the flag is completely burned.

Closing Song: "God Bless America"
Closing Prayer:

Afterward, remove the rivets and bury them or place them in a lake.

Unique Ways to Certify

Encouraging young women to certify can sometimes be a trying process. There are those girls who jump right in and have no problem getting their hands dirty. Others, it seems, need to be pushed along the entire way. Putting in place a regular reward process can help tremendously. You can give out camp necklaces, charm bracelets, food rewards, or certificates. Church Distribution has reward certificates that are designed to be handed out each year. Use these! It helps the girls realize that they really are accomplishing something that is not easy. It takes time and dedication to certify. A certificate in their scrapbooks each year will be a great reminder of camp and all the wonderful experiences they had.

Hiking

When taking a group of girls hiking, it may help some leaders and girls to have stations along the way. These stations can serve as a resting point and also as a teaching tool. You can take this time at each station to teach a topic relating to your camp theme. It is fun to have members of the ward or stake Young Women presidency as the teachers. You could also use members of the stake presidency. Teaching while hiking will make it seem more exciting to those girls who would otherwise not enjoy themselves.

Recycling

What better time to teach your young women about recycling and protecting the environment than at camp. To do an easy recycling activity, have three garbage cans at your camp—one for burnables, one for non-burnables, and one for recyclables. The burnable garbage can be used to start fires. Make sure this garbage can gets emptied by burning its contents daily. The non-burnable will either need to be carried out or taken by the camp garbage collector. The recyclables garbage can be taken to a recycling center upon returning home from camp. You go through so much trash at camp, why not teach about recycling during the process?

Scripture Study

Every level of certification requires the young women to read fifteen minutes in the scriptures daily while at camp. Why not set aside a time each day for this? Sometimes we get so caught up in our other fun and goofy activities, we forget to leave time for the spiritual moments. This should be a time when the camp is quiet and no other activities are allowed. You can also combine with other activities to include scripture study time. While gathering for breakfast, have a mini devotional. Then after everyone eats, they can read the scriptures. Take advantage of the times when you have all your young women gathered. This is a perfect time to study individually. Then open it up for questions or discussion.

Lashing

How fun would it be to lash a chair for your bishop to sit on during his visit to Girls Camp? Or to give as a gift to your ward or stake camp director? Have a contest—see who can think up the most creative chair or stool. Who can lash the fastest? You could lash a mat to be placed at the front door of the cabin, tent, or lodge.

Camp Necklace

The necklace is a brief summary of camp. You want the young women to be able to look at it and remember their experiences. Make sure it accomplishes this goal. If you are just starting a camp necklace tradition, give one to every girl in all camp levels. In the future, only the new first years and other new girls will need one. The girls will use the same necklace for all of their years at camp and simply add to it each year. The girls can wear these necklaces all year long to show off their accomplishments at camp. Below are instructions for making a camp necklace, along with a picture of a completed necklace.

1. Start with a piece of thinly sliced wood (½-inch thick). Cherry or apple tree branches are the perfect size (1½-inch wide circle)
2. Drill a hole in the piece of wood so string can be inserted through it to form a necklace. Use hefty string since this will eventually be holding lots of goodies.
3. Each year as the girls pass off their certification requirements, they will receive beads, one for each certification requirement completed. Do not hand out beads until all certification requirements are met, and don't hand out two beads if they only pass off two requirements. The young woman either receives all her beads or none.
4. Decide on a different color of bead for each year up through the fourth year. Pick colors that will go well together; get either all solid-colored beads or all opaque colored beads. For the YCL years, give different shaped beads, such as hearts or circles.

First Year: Orange
Second Year: Yellow
Third Year: Clear or white
Fourth Year: Blue
YCL Years: One red bead, round or shaped

5. On the final day, present the young women who have passed off all their certification with their beads. Make this a big event. The young women love to show off their accomplishments to their leaders, so let them.

6. To encourage the girls to attend every year, hand out a heart-shaped bead in a value color in addition to the certification beads. When they have gone all seven years (or hand out two in their final year as a sixth year) they will have a heart bead in each of the value colors.

7. In addition to the beads, shrinky dinks are a fun addition to the camp necklace. These are made for all sorts of different activities. These can be made for the camp theme, skits, flag, canoeing, swimming, or whatever activities you do at your camp. Go overboard and the girls will remember!

5 Spiritual Aspect

Spiritual activities at camp take a lot of inspiration and dedication. They need to be planned carefully. You want to provide every opportunity you can to let your young women feel the Spirit. When you are planning spiritual activities, make them short so that they aren't overwhelming.

These suggestions are great starting points. Plan with the Spirit and tweak these activities to fit the needs of your young women. And make sure to always let the Spirit be felt through your presence and example.

Spiritual Hike

Go to an area that is not in your campground. Have the girls sit on blankets while listening to a five- to ten-minute devotional. Some topic suggestions are prayer, dating appropriately, chastity, eternal families, temple endowments, serving others, Young Women values, the Second Coming, scripture stories, Personal Progress, the sacrament, and so forth. After the devotional, let the girls sit quietly for fifteen to thirty minutes to ponder, pray, study scriptures, and write in their journals.

Land of Destiny

This is a little hike that involves planning and extra people. Set up stations along your hiking path. Each station can represent a stage in a young woman's life (birth, baptism, high school graduation, mission, marriage, children, grandchildren, death, spirit world). At each station, set up a scene; you will need to bring in children and adults of the appropriate ages to create some of the scenes (be sure to get approval by your stake, if needed). Play soft music relevant to each scene; for instance, play "Pomp and Circumstance" at the graduation scene. Have a narrator read a prepared script (just a paragraph or two) at each station that tells the young women about each stage and its importance. At the last station (spirit world) talk about eternal families.

Campfires

These should be held every evening at camp. Start by singing some fun, upbeat camp songs, then a few more spiritual songs. Begin each campfire with an opening prayer and a spiritual thought or a scripture. Then have a YCL give a short devotional, ending with her testimony. Close with a song and a prayer. Stay and sing around the campfire. This is a good environment in which to feel the Spirit and increase unity among your ward or group.

Testimony Meeting

Have a testimony meeting on the last night of camp. Invite the bishopric and their wives up for this meeting. Obviously you should not force anyone to bear their testimony. Allow them to volunteer because they want to. Encourage them to bear their testimony, and be an example, but let the Spirit guide the young women. Be sure to invite the bishopric members to share their testimonies as well.

A Letter from Home

Invite the parents to write a letter to their daughter, and collect these before camp. On the last night of camp, following testimony meeting, hand out these letters. The parents can express their love for their daughter and her part in their family, among other things. Make sure each letter is in a sealed envelope with the girl's name on front.

Spiritual Thoughts and Handouts

Below are a few simple, yet wonderful thoughts that can be used as daily reminders of who we are and why we are here. Each day, place a new thought on each girl's pillow, along with a little treat.

- Popularity comes from pleasing people, but greatness comes from pleasing God.
- God gave us free agency, and then he gave us the commandments to keep us free.

- I will remain free by choosing good over evil, and I will accept responsibility for my choices.
- "Till I die I will not remove mine integrity from me."—Job 27:5
- No one ever injured his eyesight by looking on the bright side of things.
- So what if God created man before woman . . . We all know that you make a rough draft before creating a masterpiece.
- Stick together and stand tall!
- Let your love be felt.
- If you believe in yourself enough and know what you want—you're gonna make it happen!
- To make your dreams come true . . . Wake up!
- There are two kinds of people in this world . . . Those we love, and those we don't know.
- We are daughters of our Heavenly Father, who loves us, and we love Him.
- Happiness is a grateful heart.
- He can only guide your footsteps when you move your feet.
- Be yourself—you're special.
- Parents are "beary" special. They give us joy and hope. (The treat can be gummy bears.)
- Do you want to have a "beary" nice day? One that's nice in every way? Well, live each day and do your part. And you'll love life with all your heart.
- No man has a good enough memory to be a successful liar.
- "A religion that does not require the sacrifice of all things never has power sufficient to produce the faith necessary to lead unto life and salvation."—Joseph Smith
- When life doesn't seem like a bed of roses, remember who wore the thorns.
- If you can't stand your problems . . . try kneeling.
- Don't ask the Lord for a lighter burden . . . Ask for a stronger back.
- Rise up and soar to great heights—we are heaven bound.
- Remember the source of all light—Christ.
- If you meet someone who can't smile, give them one of yours.
- Worry is like a rocking horse, it keeps you going but gets you nowhere.
- "Life is fragile and, therefore, should be handled with prayer."—Harold B. Lee

- It's nice to be important, but it's more important to be nice.
- Learn from the mistakes of others. You could never live long enough to make them all yourself.
- Quality is never an accident. It is always the result of intelligent effort.
- Remembrance:
  I won't forget my days with you;
  Your memory will not leave my view.
  For you have changed my life, you see
  And in my heart you'll always be.
  Your friendship is my greatest prize.
  It warms my heart like summer skies.
  In darkest moments of the night,
  Your friendship brings a guided light.
  And now I see through all my tears
  I'll never lose you through the years;
  No matter what, we'll never part,
  For I have locked you in my heart.
  —Ernie Elliott

Young Women Values at Camp

The Young Women values are so important in the lives of the young women you serve. They will provide a constant reminder of who they are and why they are here.

Faith	I am a daughter of a Heavenly Father who loves me, and I will have faith in his Eternal plan, which centers in Jesus Christ, my Savior. (D&C 14:7)	White
Divine Nature	I have inherited divine qualities which I will strive to develop. (2 Peter 1:4–7)	Blue

Individual Worth	I am of infinite worth with my own divine mission, which I will strive to fulfill. (D&C 18:10)	Red
Knowledge	I will continually seek opportunities for learning and growth. (D&C 88:118)	Green
Choice and Accountability	I will remain free by choosing good over evil and will accept responsibility for my choices. (Joshua 24:15)	Orange
Good Works	I will nurture others and build the kingdom through righteous service. (3 Nephi 2:16)	Yellow
Integrity	I will have the moral courage to make my actions consistent with my knowledge of right and wrong. (Job 27:5)	Purple

Journal Sheets

Provide a colored journal sheet for each value. On each sheet have the following questions:

- What did I learn about the value?
- Why is this value important to me?
- How can I improve it in my life?
- What is my commitment to live this value?

Camp Pillow Case

At the beginning of camp, give each girl a white pillow case. Throughout the week, instruct each girl to look for a value that she admires in each girl in their ward or group. Have them write on that girl's pillow case with a permanent marker of the color of that value. For example: "I admire you, Shannon, because of your *good works* in always doing things without being asked" (written in yellow ink).

Value-Centered Scriptures

Have the girls look up scriptures that pertain to each value and then mark them with the colored pencil that corresponds to the value color.

Value Bracelets

Assign each ward or group a value. Give each group a cloth or leather bracelet that represents the color of their value.

Value Walk

Prepare eight stations along a path or in eight different groves of trees. Teach one value at each station through stories or analogies. Rotate every five minutes. At the last station, discuss how the Young Women values can help us return to our Father in Heaven and how they can lead us down the path of righteousness.

Daily Values

Choose a different value each day for all the wards or groups can focus on. Dress in the value color. Prepare foods that represent the color. Use scripture references to reinforce the importance of the value. Memorize the definition, scripture, and color for the value. Try and help the girls see values in everything around them.

Value Campfire

At most fireplace stores or wood-burning stove companies, you can buy fire crystals that turn the fire colors when thrown onto a fire. You can also buy specific chemicals that turn colors when burned: potassium—purple, sodium—orange, lithium—pink, barium or copper—green, calcium—red, lead—blue, road-flare powder—pink (break open the stick and place on wood; it will ignite when heated to a hot enough temperature). Granulated sugar and coffee creamer mixed together makes sparks for a few seconds after being tossed into the fire. *Be sure to use extreme caution when using any type of chemical near a fire.*

Scriptures

The scriptures provide an endless number of verses that pertain to each value. Use these to plan any activity centered around the Young Women values.

Value Quotes

Quotes seem to stick with young women better than most lessons.

Faith

- A friend once wrote: "Give me your faith not your doubts."
- "Now faith is the substance of things hoped for, the evidence of things not seen."—Hebrews 11:1

Divine Nature

- "Those who are at war with others are not at peace with themselves."—William Hazlitt

Individual Worth

- "Remember the worth of souls is great in the sight of God."—D&C 18:10

Knowledge

- "Education is the power to think clearly, the power to act well in the world's work, and the power to appreciate life."—Brigham Young

Choice and Accountability

- "Sin is not hurtful because it is forbidden, but it is forbidden because it is hurtful."—Benjamin Franklin

Good Works

- "Those who bring sunshine to others, cannot keep it from themselves."—Sir James Barnei

Integrity

- "Character is much easier kept than recovered."—Thomas Paine

Value Stories

The list of books below all contain "value-able" lessons that can be taught and applied into the lives of your young women. You may choose to have a bedtime story every night to reiterate the seven Young Women values.

A Bad Case of Stripes	David Shannon
A Big Fat Enormous Lie	Marjorie Weinman Sharmat
A Grandmother's Story	Glenn Halak
All I Really Need to Know I Learned in Kindergarten	Robert Fulghum
All the Mama's	Carol Schough
All the Places to Love	Patricia MacLachlan
The Aminal	Lorna Balian
Babushka's Doll	Patricia Polacco
The Carrot Seed	Ruth Krauss
Edward the Emu	Sheena Knowles
Empty Pot	Demi
The Enchanted Wood	Ruth Sanderson
Everybody Needs a Rock	Byrd Baylor
Fanny's Dream	Caralyn Buehner
The Grouchy Ladybug	Eric Carle
Glimpses	Marjorie Hinckley and Virginia Pearce
Hailstones and Halibut Bones	Mary O'Neill
I Wish I Were a Butterfly	James Howe
I'm In Charge of Celebrations	Byrd Baylor
Just A Little Bit	Ann Tompert
The Keeping Quilt	Patricia Polacco
The Little Brute Family	Russel and Lillian Hoban
The Little Engine That Could	Watty Piper
Magical Hands	Marjorie Barker
Miss Rumphius	Barbara Cooney
Mufaro's Beautiful Daughters	John Steptoe
My House Has Stars	Megan McDonald
No, David	David Shannon
Oh, the Places You'll Go	Dr. Seuss
Once There Were Giants	Martin Waddel
The Paper Bag Princess	Robert Munsch

Pelle's New Suit	Elsa Beskorv
People	Peter Spier
Petunia	Roger Duvoisin
Play With Me	Marie Hall Ets
Quick as a Cricket	Audrey Wood
The Rag Coat	Lauren Mills
The Rainbabies	Laura Krauss Melmed
The Selfish Giant	Oscar Wilde
Seven Blind Mice	Ed Young
Shoemaker Martin	Leo Tolstoy
The Sneetches	Dr. Seuss
Somewhere Today	Bert Kitchen
Sylvester and the Magic Pebble	William Steig
Tacky the Penguin	Helen Lester
They Were Strong and Good	Robert Lawson
The Treasure	Uri Schulevitz
Two of Everything	Lily Toy Hong
What You Know First	Patricia Maclachlan
You Are Special	Max Lucado

# Fun

Fun—that's what it's all about. Include some of these ideas as you plan your fun-filled week of camp.

Secret Sisters

Having secret sisters is a fun addition to the regular friendship-building activities at camp. Each young woman draws or is assigned a name of another young woman attending camp. While at camp, they give a little note and a small gift to their secret sister every day. The gifts should not be expensive. Something homemade is always nice. Have the girls reveal their identity on the last night of camp. Each girl could fill out a questionnaire about herself and then give a page of it to her secret sister each day. The questionnaires could be on cute stationery with some fun facts such as these:

Tell your secret sister . . .
1. Something you keep under your bed.
2. Something you are afraid of.
3. What your favorite color is.
4. What your favorite scripture is and why.
5. What temple you want to get married in and why.

Rainy Day Box

Having a rainy day box for camp will come in handy more than once. These activities can be used for rainy days, hot days, if a young woman gets injured and needs to stay in bed, or those days when there is too much free time (which never happens at camp, does it?). You can include some of the following items in your box:

crayons	scissors	glue or glue sticks
colored pencils	envelopes	coloring books
markers	travel games	pens and pencils
pencils and pens	old scriptures	blank papers
jacks	checkers	construction paper
bingo	rope	small noisemakers
jump ropes	cotton balls	hair accessories
hymn books	yarn	wooden sticks
camp song books	stickers	Polaroid camera and film
rulers	stapler	CDs of kids' songs
candy	tape	small CD player

Use your imagination on what to do with all these items. Add your own ideas. You can have drawing contests and coloring contests, a scripture chase, play charades, sing hymns, have a checker competition, play beauty parlor, write letters to your ward missionaries, and so forth. You will never be sorry to have this on hand.

Steal the Flag

Steal the Flag is usually played on a stake level. Each ward has a flag that represents their ward theme. Each flag needs to be made of some durable material. The flags are then placed on a pole. PVC pipe works best. The object of the game is to see which ward can steal the most flags from the other wards during the week.

Each night at the stake flag ceremony, have each ward report how many flags they have (of other wards) and which ward still has their original flag. At the end of the day return the flags to their original ward. At the end of the week, the ward who had stolen the most flags and the ward who never got their flag stolen, win. The main purpose of this game is, of course, fun! If it gets out of hand or if you feel there is too much competitive spirit, call it quits.

The rules of the game are:
1. Your flag *should* be guarded continually.
2. When you are touching or holding your flag, it can't be taken.

3. When someone sees that your flag is unguarded, they can make their move.
4. When you see your flag being taken, accept defeat for that day.
5. You can try to retrieve your flag after it has been stolen and before the evening report.
6. Your stake may want to set rules as to when flags can or can't be taken (during hikes, during devotionals, after lights out, and so forth).
7. A hint: Putting your flag in a #10 can with cement holding up the pole makes it harder for the other wards to carry it away.

Camp Awards

Listed below are some awards that can be handed out at camp. Try to come up with more depending on the activities you do at your camp.

- Skits: Most Creative, Most Gospel-Centered Theme, Best Costume, Worst Costume, Most Creative Gospel Application, Best Use of Your Young Women, Best Dance, Best Song.

- Water Activities: Wettest, Best Paddler, Driest, Tipping the Boat, Future Sailor.

- Hiking: Future Forest Ranger, Leader of the Pack, Hiking Stick, Best Gear, Worst Gear, Camel (water drinker), "Are We Almost There?" Bravery in the Field, Preparedness in the Field.

- Campground: Neatest Campground, Messiest Campground, Best Decorations, Most Creative Decorations, Best Use of Space, Fire Pit, Chef, Make Yourself at Home, Dog Wood, Gopher, Honey Bee, Stinger, Fire Builder, Pyro, Wood Chuck, Always on Time, Never on Time.

- Friendship or Spiritual: Prayerful, Scriptorian, Happy Helper, President.

- Archery: Best Aim, Worst Aim, Bull's Eye, Needs Target Practice.

Secret Ward

Having a secret ward at camp can really help enforce the wonderful opportunity of service. Choose a ward in your stake that you feel would benefit from little acts of kindness all week long. This can be a ward that has only a few young women or a lot. It may be a group of girls who need a little extra encouragement or attention. You may choose to surprise more than one ward during the week. To do this, all you need is a little imagination and you're ready. Let the girls take the lead when performing the service. Here are some ideas of ways to surprise your secret ward:

- Give the ward a treat, such as marshmallow popcorn, skittles, cookies, rolls, or candy.
- Do little acts of kindness, such as start their fire so when they return it will be nice and hot, sweep out their cabin or tent, start a pot of hot water and leave some hot cocoa packets.
- Make little treasures for everyone in the ward, such as prayer rocks, prayer rugs, necklaces, goodie bags, and bath salts.
- Deliver their surprise unannounced. This can be done when their campsite is empty or while they are there.

Top Ten Lists

A top ten list is always a favorite at camp. It is just a funny, light-hearted list of the day's inside jokes. The girls usually come up with the list as wards or groups. You can schedule this into your evening campfire, but do make sure to do it at the beginning so you don't interrupt the spiritual moments that usually occur toward the end of the evening. Here is an example of what a top ten list could be:

Things Overheard at Camp

10. What about Kurt and Jessica?
9. You're killing me, Smalls!
8. Who made out in the rain?
7. Are these bat droppings in my bed?
6. Thanks, *For the Strength of Youth* Woman!
5. Who's Kaleb?
4. Please, doesn't anyone have any toilet paper?
3. Don't worry, I taped *Survivor* last night!
2. Am I fat?
1. Have you seen Sister Wible in the morning?

Skits

As part of the camp certification process, first and fourth years must help plan and present a skit. This is a great time to discover your young women's hidden talents. Skits can be so fun and easy if you let the girls decide what to do. When planning a skit, keep it simple and easy to remember. Below are some skit preparation ideas.

Fairy Tales and Stories

- Mary Had a Little Lamb: From the lamb's point of view, he was loyal!
- Hansel and Gretel: Be strong enough to do what is right even in the face of danger.
- Humpty Dumpty: If he had been stronger, he wouldn't have broken. What commandment will break you?
- The Boy Who Cried Wolf: Honesty.
- Beauty and the Beast: Look on the heart. We all have "beastly" qualities that need to be tamed.
- Mulan: Honor your father and mother. Look for who you really are. Mushu can act as the Holy Ghost.
- The Wizard of Oz: Stay on the right path, choose your friends wisely, and look inside yourself to find your own spiritual strength.

Skit in a Bag

The Skit-in-a-Bag approach is an alternative to preparing skits ahead of time. Each group is given a list of items in the bag. They must present a skit using only the items in the bag. Give them the list of items a day or two ahead of time. You may want to assign each group a general theme for their skit (one of the six Be's, modesty, one of the Young Women values, a book or a story, and so forth).

Here are some possible items to be put into a Skit Bag. Have the bag of items available the day of the skits for the wards to look through and to get a feel for what they can use. The wards will take turns using the skit bag when it is their ward's turn to present a skit. Pick and choose which ones would work the best for what you want to see happen. Remind them that only these items may be used in their skits!

large blanket	rolling pin	rolled-up newspaper
pirate hat	hair dryer	picture of Christ
baseball cap	old dress	wooden dagger and shield
cane	baby doll	small teddy bear
shawl	angel halo	cell phone
devil horns	scarf	fun hat

bandana	cape	*For the Strength of Youth*
rope	sorcerer's hat	poncho
headbands	earmuffs	pioneer bonnet
farmer's hat	sleeping mat	curlers
lipstick	towel	microphone feather duster

Helpful Hints

- Children's books can make great stories for skits.
- The scriptures are a great resource. There are so many wonderful stories and positive examples that can be taken from them.
- The *For the Strength of Youth* booklet is another wonderful resource.
- Be sure that you set a time limit to how long the skits should be; three to five minutes is plenty. No one likes sitting through a boring ten-minute skit. You may choose to set a timer. If so, pull the group off the stage with a cane when the timer goes off.
- Be sure to set some ground rules before presenting the skits. No one wants to come away with hurt feelings.
- You may want to have some entertainment planned between skits while the next ward or group prepares.
- Skits that involve the crowd are always welcome.
- Hand out awards at the end of the evening.

Crafts

Crafts at camp can be a welcome break from the other rigorous activities. They also bring out the artistic side in everyone. Always try out crafts at home before camp. These instructions are for home. You can change them according to your camping situation. You will most likely not have a microwave oven at camp, so use your camp stove or hot coals in its place. For crafts that involve painting, cover tables with butcher paper for easy cleanup. Be sure to have enough paint brushes, among other things, so more than a few girls can do their crafts at one time. Here are just a few suggestions:

first-aid kits	waterproof patches	refrigerator magnet thoughts
mirror silhouettes	cross-stitch	friendship bracelets
prayer rocks	hairbands	popsicle or wood puzzles
latch hook	beaded bandanas	camp theme decorations
glycerin soaps	baby quilts	Young Women stationery
candy bar cards	lip gloss	painted wooden objects

You could also paint a book of remembrance chart with water colors. These can include the young woman's birthday, baptism, and any other special events. Another idea is to lash a small garbage can or door mat for your tent or cabin.

Bath Salts

4 cups Epson salt
1 Tbsp. glycerin
food coloring
perfume samples

Mix in a bowl. Add your choice of coloring and perfume. Keep in a bag with raffia tied around top or in a small jar with a fabric-covered lid. Enjoy a soothing bath upon returning home from camp.

Bath Fizzies

1 cup baking soda
⅓ cup citric acid
witch hazel in a spray bottle
15 drops of scent
food coloring

Mix baking soda and citric acid together in a bowl. Put in about 15 drops of scent and food coloring. Start spraying witch hazel lightly into mixture while forming balls. Stop adding witch hazel when mixture begins clumping and holding together and feels cool to the touch. Do not add too much or else mixture will flatten and not form. Form into balls or place in molds. Let dry overnight. Add to a bath and enjoy. Makes 5 large balls.

Strawberry Cream Glycerin Soap

1 pound white glycerin soap base
1 tsp. sugar
4 Tbsp. sweet almond oil
2 drops of red coloring
5 drops strawberry fragrance oil
10 drops vanilla fragrance oil

Melt glycerin in microwave. Add sugar, almond oil, color, and fragrance. Stir until mixed. Pour into molds. Cool. You could also make orange cream by substituting orange essential oil and color for the strawberry.

Basic Lip Gloss

2 Tbsp. petroleum jelly
1 tsp. beeswax
10–14 drops essential oil

In a small pot, melt the petroleum jelly; then add beeswax. When melted, remove from heat and add essential oil. Pour into a container and let cool. You can add any oil-based coloring or flavoring that you desire.

Helpful hints: There are a few different containers that work well for storing the lip gloss in: film canisters, prescription bottles, "dressing on the side" containers, or any other small containers. Another great container is from the candy sprinkles that come out around the holidays. You can find lip gloss ingredients at craft stores, health food stores, or on the Internet.

Chocolate Lip Gloss

3 Tbsp. cocoa butter
4–5 chocolate chips
1 liquid capsule vitamin E

Melt together; blend ingredients with a spoon until smooth. Place in a container and refrigerate until solid.

Quote Plaques

paint
flat, thin pieces of wood (heart, square, circle, oval, house)
markers
magnets

Paint the wood and allow to dry. Write a quote on the front with markers. Place a small magnet on the back.

Picture Frames

paint
plain, unpainted wooden frames
decorations (foam, puff paint, glitter, pom-poms)

Paint the frames and allow to dry before decorating. The girls can put a picture from camp in their frame.

Value Blocks

paint
square wooden blocks (7 per girl)
markers

Paint each block a value color. Write the value name that corresponds with the color. Stack these in a row, displayed on a dresser.

Value Color Sheet

crayons, markers, colored pencils
picture to color

Young women love to color! Find a picture that would be easy to color, and make copies. Try to find pictures that could incorporate the values or value colors.

(7) Camp Songs

A camp song book can be a good way to help the girls learn the songs, especially if some girls know slightly different versions of the songs. You can start your camp song book by using the songs in this section. To listen to Girls Camp songs, go to www.ywsuggestions.net.

My Country 'Tis of Thee

My country 'tis of thee, sweet land of liberty, of thee I sing.
Land where my fathers died, land of the pilgrims pride,
From every mountainside, let freedom ring.

My native country thee, land of the noble free, thy name I love.
I love the rocks and rills, thy woods and temples hills.
My heart with rapture thrills, like that above.

Let music swell the breeze, and ring from all the trees, sweet freedom's song;
Let mortal tongues awake, let all that breathe partake,
Let rocks their silence break, the sound prolong.

Our father's God, to thee, Author of liberty, to thee we sing.
Long may our land be bright, with freedom's holy light.
Protect us by thy might, Great God, our King!

America, America

America, America,
Can we tell you how we feel?
You have given us your treasures;
We love you so.

*Sing once as a group, then in a round as two groups. Second group begins after
first group has sung "America, America." Each group sings entire song twice.*

America the Beautiful

Oh, beautiful for spacious skies, for amber waves of grain.
For purple mountains majesties, above the fruited plains!
America! America! God shed his grace on thee.
And crowned thy good with brotherhood, from sea to shining sea.

Oh, beautiful for pilgrim feet, whose stern impassioned stress
A thorough-fare of freedom beat across the wilderness!
America! America! God mend thy every flaw,
Confirm thy soul in self-control, thy liberty in law.

Oh, beautiful for heroes proved, in liberating strife.
Who more than self their country loved, and mercy more than life!
America! America! May God thy gold refine
Till all success is nobleness, and every gain divide.

Oh, beautiful for patriot dream, that sees beyond the years.
Thine alabaster cities gleam, undimmed by human tears!
America! America! God shed his grace on thee.
And crowned thy good with brotherhood, from sea to shining sea.

Star-Spangled Banner

O say, can you see, by the dawn's early light,
What so proudly we hailed at the twilight's last gleaming,
Whose broad stripes and bright stars, through the perilous fight,
O'er the ramparts we watched, were so gallantly streaming?
And the rockets' red glare, the bombs bursting in air,
Gave proof through the night that our flag was still there.
O say, does that star-spangled banner yet wave
O'er the land of the free, and the home of the brave?

Battle Hymn of the Republic

Mine eyes have seen the glory of the coming of the Lord.
He is trampling out the vintage where the grapes of wrath are stored;
He hath loosed the fateful lightening of his terrible swift sword;
His truth is marching on.

Chorus:
Glory, glory, Hallelujah! Glory, glory, Hallelujah!
Glory, glory, Hallelujah! His truth is marching on.

He has sounded forth the trumpet that will never call retreat.
He is sifting out the hearts of men before His judgement seat.
Oh be swift my soul to answer Him, be jubilant my feet!
Our God is marching on! (Chorus)

In the beauty of the lilies, Christ was born across the sea,
With the glory in His bosom that transfigures you and me
As He died to make men holy, let us live to make men free
While God is marching on. (Chorus)

Spider's Web

Low

There's a web like a spider's web
Made of silver light and shadow
Spun by the moon in my room last night
It's a web made to catch a dream
Hold it fast till I awaken
As if to tell me my dream is of you

High

It's a web like a spider's web
Spun by the moon in my room last night
It's a web made to catch a dream
As if to tell me my dream is of you.

Sung in a round.

I Will Stand

I will stand for truth and righteousness.
I will seek the light.
I will hold my torch for all to see.
My torch is the light of Christ.

Sung in a round.

Edelweiss

Edelweiss, Edelweiss, every morning you greet me.
Small and white, clean and bright.
You look happy to greet me.
Blossoms of snow, may you bloom and grow, bloom and grow forever.
Edelweiss, Edelweiss, bless my homeland forever.

Shalom Song

Shalom, Ha va rim, Shalom, Ha va rim, Sha-lom
E lee tra a low, E lee tra a low, Sha-lom

Friends

Friends are nothing till they sing together;
They must sing all day,
They must sing the night away,
They must sing together,
They must sing.

1. sing
2. work
3. play
4. laugh
5. "Friends are nothing till they part with tear drops in their eyes, they must go their separate ways, and they hope to meet again someday."

Bless Our Camp

Bless our camp, bless our friends.
Come, oh Lord, and be with us.
May our year bring us peace;
Send your love to surround us.

Friendship and peace,
May they bloom and grow, bloom and grow forever.
Bless our camp, bless our friends,
Bless our friendships forever.

Sung to the tune of Edelweiss.

Make New Friends

Make new friends,
But keep the old.
One is silver,
And the other gold.

Sung in a round.

I Love the Mountains

I love the mountains, I love the rolling hills,
I love the fountains, I love the daffodils,
I love the fireside, when all the lights are low,
Boom-dee-ah-da Boom-dee-ah-da
Boom-dee-ah-da Boom-dee-ah-da Boom!

Sung in a four-part round.

Mormon Boy

I know a Mormon boy.
He is my pride and joy.
He knows most everything
From Alma on down.
Someday I'll be his wife;
We'll have Eternal life.
Oh, how I love that Mormon boy.

Actions: slap own legs twice, slap left leg and [left] neighbor's right leg twice, slap own legs twice, slap right leg and [right] neighbor's left leg twice, slap own legs once, slap left leg and [left] neighbor's right leg once, slap own legs once, slap right leg and [right] neighbo'rs left leg once, slap own legs once, clap, snap fingers next to head.

Catalina Madalina

Chorus:

Catalina Madalina Ruebensteiner, Wallensteiner, Hoken, Pokem,
   Moken was her name.

She had a funny smell, and she had a funny name.
She got it from her mother by the same, same, same. (Chorus)

She had two hairs on the top of her head.
The dog-gone things were carrot red. (Chorus)

She had two eyes with which to see.
One looked at you while the other looked at me. (Chorus)

She had two holes in the middle of her nose.
One stayed open while the other stayed closed. (Chorus)

She had two ears like the sails on a boat.
Her Adam's apple bobbed up and down her throat. (Chorus)

She had two teeth in the middle of her mouth.
one pointed north and the other pointed south. (Chorus)

She had a wart on the end of her chin.
She said it was a dimple, but a dimple turns in. (Chorus)

She had two hands with which to eat.
The dog-gone things were as big as her feet. (Chorus)

She had a shape like a hairy ape.
Held together like Scotch brand tape. (Chorus)

She had a peculiar smell to her feet.
Smelled like a skunk in a quick retreat. (Chorus)

If rain makes flowers sweet and clean,
There ought to be a cloudburst on Madalene. (Chorus)

Noah Song

The Lord said to Noah, "There's gonna be a floody floody."
Lord said to Noah, "There's gonna be a floody floody.
Get those animals out of the muddy muddy,
Children of the Lord."

Chorus:
So rise and shine and give God your glory, glory.
Rise and shine and give God your glory, glory.
Rise and shine and give God your glory, glory,
Children of the Lord.

The Lord said to Noah, "You'd better build an arky arky."
Lord said to Noah, "You'd better build an arky arky.
Build it out of hickory barky barky,
Children of the Lord." (Chorus)

The animals, they came on, they came on by twosies, twosies.
Animals, they came on, they came on by twosies, twosies.
Elephants and kangaroosies, roosies,
Children of the Lord. (Chorus)

It rained and poured for forty daysies, daysies.
Rained and poured for forty daysies, daysies.
Nearly drove those animals crazy, crazy,
Children of the Lord. (Chorus)

The sun came out and dried up the landy, landy.
Sun came out and dried up the landy, landy.
Everything was fine and dandy, dandy,
Children of the Lord. (Chorus)

The animals, they came off, they came off by threesies, threesies.
Animals they came off, they came off by threesies, threesies.
All thanks to the birds and beezies, beezies,
Children of the Lord. (Chorus)

So this is the end of the end of our story story.
This is the end of the end of our story story.
Everything was hunky dory dory,
Children of the Lord. (Chorus)

Ha ha ha, we fooled you, you thought it was over over.
Ha ha, we fooled you, you thought it was over over.
Now we start the whole thing over over,
Children of the Lord. (Chorus)

Birds in the Wilderness

Here we sit like
Birds in the wilderness,
Birds in the wilderness,
Birds in the wilderness.

Here we sit like
Birds in the wilderness
Waiting for the rest to come.
Waiting for the rest to come
Waiting for the rest to come.

Here we sit like
Birds in the wilderness
Waiting for the rest to come.

Skunk Song

Oh, I stuck my head down a little skunk's hole,
And the little skunk said, "Well bless my soul.
Take it out, take it out, take it out, take it out, remove it!"

Well, I didn't take it out, and the little skunk said,
"If you don't take it out, you'll wish you had.
Take it out, take it out, take it out, take it out, remove it!"
Pssssstt! I removed it too late!

Girls Camp

The weather down at Girls Camp they say is mighty fine.
The rain is always pouring the sun will never shine.

Chorus:
Oh, Gee, I wanna go to Girls Camp.
Gee, mom, I wanna go. Where do you wanna go?
Gee, mom, I wanna go to Girls Camp.

The ticks we have at Girls Camp they say are mighty fine.
One went up my pant leg. I had an awful time. (Chorus)

The biffys we have at Girls Camp they say are mighty fine.
You've never seen a girl take such a little time. (Chorus)

The bed partners we have at Girls Camp they say are mighty fine.
How the heck would you know, you haven't slept with mine. (Chorus)

The biscuits we have at Girls Camp they say are mighty fine.
One fell off the table and killed a friend of mine. (Chorus)

The hikes we take at Girls Camp they say are mighty fine.
When sliding down a glacier, you fall and crack your spine. (Chorus)

The bugler we have at Girls Camp they say is mighty fine.
She blows her horn at seven, then she sleeps in till nine. (Chorus)

The chicken we have at Girls Camp they say is mighty fine.
But once two drumsticks got up and started beating time. (Chorus)

Hanky Panky

Down by the banks of the hanky panky,
Where the bull frogs jump from bank to banky,
Singin' eep, op, ope, op, one jumps in and goes kur-plop.

Sung in a round.

A Boy and a Girl

Just a boy and a girl in a little canoe,
With the moon shining all around.
And their paddle didn't even make a sound.
Well, they talked and they talked
Till the moon went down.
He said, "You'd better kiss me or get out and swim."
So what ya gonna do in a little canoe,
When the moon is shining alla,
The moon is shining alla,
The moon is shining alla round?
Get out and swim!

Princess Pat

The princess Pat / lived in a tree.
She sailed across / the seven seas.
She sailed across / the channel too.
And brought with her / a rig-a-bamboo.

Chorus:
A rig-a-bamboo / now what is that?
It's something made / by the princess Pat.
It's red and gold / and a purple too.
That's why it's called / a rig-a-bamboo.

Now Captain Jack / had a mighty fine crew.
They sailed across / the channel too.
Their ship did sink / and so will you.
If you don't take / a rig-a-bamboo.

The group repeats after every slash and every line.

Sippin' Cider

The cutest boy / I ever saw
Was sippin' ci-/ der through a straw.
The cutest boy I ever saw was sippin' cider through a straw.

I asked him if / He'd show me how
To sip that ci-/ der though a straw.

First cheek to cheek / then jaw to jaw,
We sipped that ci-/ der through a straw.

Then all at once / that darn straw slipped
And we sipped ci-/ der lip to lip.

That's how I got / my mother-in-law
And forty-nine kids / who call me Ma.

The moral of / this story is
Don't drink your ci-/ der, drink root beer!

The group repeats after every slash and every line and then sings the entire verse together, as shown in verse one.

The Boatmen

1, 2, 3, 4, 5, 6, (pause) 7, 8!
Oh, the boatmen dance and the boatmen sing
And the boatmen do most any old thing.
When the boatmen come to shore,
They spend all their money and they work for more.
Hi, ho, the boatmen go, up and down the river of the Ohio
Hi, ho, the boatmen go, up and down the river of the Ohio
1, 2, 3, 4, 5, 6, (pause) 7, 8!

Pow Wow!

We are the red man, tall and quaint (repeat)
With our feathers and war paint (repeat)
Pow wow (repeat)
Pow wow (repeat)
We're the red men from the old gun towns.

Chorus:
We are the red men, feathers in our headband.
Down by the dead men. Ump! Pow wow

We don't like to go on hike; Muchum ride on motor bikes. (Vrrooom!)
We don't like to walk in rain; Muchum rather take the train. (Toot-toot)
We don't like to do first aid; Fingers get stuck in band-aid.
We don't like to clean the john; Makes our hands stick all day long.
We don't like to go to bed; Muchum rather party instead.
We had better end this song; Or it might last all night long.

Flea

Flea
Flea fly
Flea fly flo
Vista
Kooma-la, Kooma-la, Kooma-la Vista
On no no no, not the Vista
Eenie meenie deci-meenie, ooah-ooah-a-meenie
Ex-a-meenie, sol-s-meenie, ooah ooah
A beep billy oatin' doatin', bo-boat, ski-deetin' datin'
shhhh . . . (together)

The group repeats after every line, getting softer and softer.

The Cannibal King

The Cannibal King with the big nose ring,
Fell in love with a husky maid.
And every night by the pail moon light,
Across the bay he'd wade.

He'd hug and kiss his pretty little miss,
Under the bamboo tree.
And every night in the pail moon light
It sounded like this to me.

Chorus:
Boom, Boom (two kissing sounds)
Boom, Boom (two kissing sounds)
Under the Bamboo tree.
Boom, Boom (two kissing sounds)
Boom, Boom (two kissing sounds)
Honey, won't you marry me?

We'll build a bungalow big enough for two,
Big enough for two, my honey, big enough for one, two, three, four.
And when we're married, happy we'll be,
Under the bamboo under the bamboo tree

If you'll be M-I-N-E mine, I'll be T-H-I-N-E thine,
And I will L-O-V-E love you, all the T-I-M-E time.
You are the B-E-S-T best, of all the R-E-S-T rest,
And I'll L-O-V-E love you, all the T-I-M-E time!

I will love you all the T-I-M-E time!

Jaws

There was a story . . . doo, doo, doo, doo, doo, doo
About Jaws . . . doo, doo, doo, doo, doo, doo
About Baby Jaws . . . doo, doo, doo, doo, doo, doo
About Jr. Jaws . . . doo, doo, doo, doo, doo, doo
About Mama Jaws . . . doo, doo, doo, doo, doo, doo
About Papa Jaws . . . doo, doo, doo, doo, doo, doo
About Granny Jaws . . . doo, doo, doo, doo, doo, doo

There was a lady . . . doo, doo, doo, doo, doo, doo
A swimmin' in the sea doo, doo, doo, doo, doo, doo
There was a man . . . doo, doo, doo, doo, doo, doo
A muscle man . . . doo, doo, doo, doo, doo, doo
On, no! . . . doo, doo, doo, doo, doo, doo
Look out! . . . doo, doo, doo, doo, doo, doo
Too late! . . . doo, doo, doo, doo, doo, doo
Chomp! Chomp! . . . doo, doo, doo, doo, doo, doo

Lemon Drops and Gum Drops

If all the raindrops were lemon drops and gum drops, Oh!
What a rain that would be.

Chorus:
Standing outside with my mouth open wide.
Ah! Ah-ah! Ah! Ah-ah! Ah! Ah-ah! Ah!

If all the snowflakes were candy bars and milkshakes, Oh!
What a world this would be! (Chorus)

If all the dirt clods were hamburgers and hot dogs, Oh!
What a world this would be! (Chorus)

The Norwegian Hiker

A Norwegian hiker was hiking along
When along came a cuckoo bird interrupting his song.

Chorus:
O, la, kee, kee-e; Oh, la, ku, ku
SSShhhhhhhhhhhhhhhhhh (sound)
O, la, kee, kee-e; Oh, la, ku, ku
SSShhhhhhhhhhhhhhhhhh (sound)
O, la, kee, kee-e; Oh, la, ku, ku
SSShhhhhhhhhhhhhhhhhh (sound)
O, la, kee, kee-e; Oh, la, ku, ku

Puppy dog: Arf
Skier: Zoom
Road runner: Beep, Beep
Bear: Roar
Girl: Kiss, Kiss
Bishop: Naughty, Naughty

Father Abraham

Father Abraham had seven sons,
Seven sons had Father Abraham.
And they never laughed, and never cried,
All they did was go like this:

1. On the left (shake left hand)
2. On the right (shake right hand)
3. On the left (shake left foot)
4. On the right (shake right foot)
5. On the hips (swing hips)
6. On the head (shake head)
7. On the tongue (wag tongue)

Add one action each verse and continue doing the action throughout the song.

Aunt Came Back

Oh, my aunt came back
From Timbucktoo
And she brought with her
A wooden shoe (stomp foot)

My aunt came back
From old Algiers
And she brought with her
Some pinking shears (cut with fingers while still stomping)

Old Japan: waving fan
Country fair: rocking chair
Guadalupe: hula hoop
Timbucktoo: a nut like you!

The group repeats after every line and adds one action every verse.

I'm a Nut

I'm an acorn small and round,
Sitting on the cold, cold ground.
Nobody wants to pick me up,
Just because I am a nut!

Chorus:
I'm a nut, I'm a nut, I'm a nut, I'm a nut, I'm a nut.

Called myself on the phone,
Just to hear my golden tone.
Asked myself out for a date.
Picked me up at half past eight. (Chorus)

Took myself to the picture show,
Sat myself on the very front row.
Put my arms around my waist.
I got so fresh I slapped my face. (Chorus)

Peanut Butter—Jelly!

Chorus:

Peanut, peanut butter—jelly!
Peanut, peanut butter—jelly!

First you take the peanuts and you dig em,
Ya dig em, ya dig em, dig em, dig em.
When you get the peanuts, then you smash em,
Ya smash em, ya smash em, smash em, smash em.
Then you take the peanuts and you spread em,
Ya spread em, ya spread em, spread em, spread em. (Chorus)

First you get the berries, and you pick em,
Ya pick em, ya pick em, pick em, pick em.
Then you take the berries and you smash em,
Ya smash em, ya smash em, smash em, smash em.
Then you take the jelly and you spread it,
Ya spread it, ya spread it, spread it, spread it. (Chorus)

Then you take the sandwich and you eat it,
Ya eat it, ya eat it, eat it, eat it. (Chorus)

Is There Any Reason

Is there any reason to be in such a mood alone?
Is there any reason to be in such a mood alone?
Sitting alone on a log on a hill far away,
Sitting alone you don't find very much left to say,
La, la, la, . . .
La, la, la, . . .

Sung in a round.

On the Loose

On the loose to climb a mountain, on the loose where I am free,
On the loose to live my life the way I think my life should be
For I've only got a moment and this whole world yet to see.
I'll be looking for tomorrow on the loose.

Have you ever watched the sunrise turn the sky completely red?
Have you slept beneath the moon and stars, a pine bough for your bed?
Do you sit and talk with friends though not a word is ever said?
Then you're just like me and you've been on the loose.

There's a trail that I'll be hiking just to see where it might go.
Many places yet to visit, many people yet to know.
And in following my dreams, I will live and I will grow
On a trail that's waiting out there on the loose.

Have you ever heard a whippoorwill singing to the morning dew?
When you hear the bells ringing, do you know they ring for you?
And when you look back on the past, all I really ask
Is to remember me when you're out on the loose.

So in search of love and laughter I'll be traveling 'cross this land
Never sure of where I'm going for I haven't any plan.
And in time when you are ready, come and join me, take my hand
And together we'll share life out on the loose.

As I sit and watch the sunset and the daylight slowly fades
I am thinking of tommorow and the friendships we have made.
I will value them for always and I hope you'll do the same
And forever we'll explore life on the loose.

Midnight Train

Baby, you can't love one.
You can't love one and still have fun,
I'm leavin' on the midnight train.

Chorus:
La-de-da, oh-boy, some fun, woo-woo

Baby you can't love two.
You can't love two and still be true,
I'm leavin' on the midnight train.

Baby, you can't love three.
You can't love three and still love me,
I'm leavin' on the midnight train.

Baby, you can't love four.
You can't love four and still want more,
I'm leavin' on the midnight train.

Baby, you can't love five.
You can't love five and still be alive,
I'm leavin' on the midnight train.

Baby, you can't love six.
You can't love six and still play tricks,
I'm leavin' on the midnight train.

Baby, you can't love seven.
You can't love seven and still get to heaven,
I'm leavin' on the midnight train.

Baby, you can't love eight.
You can't love eight and play it straight,
I'm leavin' on the midnight train.

Baby, you can't love nine.
You can't love nine and still be mine,
I'm leavin' on the midnight train.

Baby, you can't love ten.
You can't love ten so kiss me again
And forget about the midnight train.

Repeat the first line of each verse and sing the chorus after each verse.

I'm Going Crazy

Chorus:

I'm going crazy;
Why don't you come along?
I must be crazy
To sing this song!

Once there was a little dog
And all she ate were cans,
And when her little puppies came,
They came in white Trans Ams!

Once there was a little cat
And all she ate was yarn,
And when her little kittens came,
They came with sweaters on!

Mary had a little lamb,
The doctor was surprised,
But when old McDonald had a farm,
The doctor nearly died!

Sing the chorus after each verse.

The Bear

The other day, / I met a bear
In tennis shoes, / a dandy pair.
The other day I met a bear in tennis shoes, a dandy pair.

He said to me, / "Why don't you run,
Because you ain't / got any gun?"

And so I ran / away from there,
But right behind / me was that bear.

Ahead of me, / I saw a tree,
A great big tree, / Oh glory be!

The nearest branch / was ten feet up.
I'd have to jump / and trust my luck.

And so I jumped / into the air,
But I missed that branch, / a way up there.

Now don't you fret; / now don't you frown,
'Cause I caught that branch / on the way back down.

The moral of / this story is,
Don't talk to bears / in tennis shoes.

That's all there is; / there ain't no more.
So what the heck / are you singing for?

The group repeats after every slash and every line and then sings the entire verse together, as shown in verse one. Sung to the tune of "Sippin' Cider."

Some Other Songs to Include

Love One Another
Love Is Spoken Here
We Thank Thee, O God, for a Prophet
I Am a Child of God
The Spirit of God
Joseph Smith's First Prayer
Somewhere Out There
Carry on
I Wonder When He Comes Again
Come, Come Ye Saints
Walk Tall, You're a Daughter of God
Because I Have Been Given Much
God Be with You
How Great Thou Art
This Land Is Your Land
God Bless America
You Are My Sunshine
Sing Your Way Home
One Tin Soldier
God Bless the USA
Kumbaya

About the Author

Vickie Hacking was raised in Orem, Utah. Attending Girls Camp at Camp MIA Shalom for so many years gave her a deep love for the mountains and an unshakable testimony of Girls Camp and the gospel. She is married to Carl Hacking, who keeps the family entertained with his job as a helicopter pilot. They have two sons, Andrew and Hunter, and two daughters, Jasmine and Hailey. Vickie is currently serving in Young Women with her daughter Jasmine.

Vickie spends most of her day cleaning house, cooking delicious food, and managing her LDS website: www.lds-yw.com.

Vickie has served in a variety of Church callings, including camp director, Young Women counselor, Young Women advisor, and Young Women sports director.

Vickie would love to hear about your Girls Camp experiences. You can contact her at ywbooks@yahoo.com.